Early Childhood Education:
Perspectives on Change

Early Childhood Education:

Perspectives on Change

Evelyn Weber
Wheelock College

Charles A. Jones Publishing Company
Worthington, Ohio

 Charles A. Jones Publishing Company, Worthington, Ohio 43085, a division of Wadsworth Publishing Company, Inc.

3 4 5 6 7 8 9 10 / 74 73 72

International Standard Book Number: 0-8396-8500

Library of Congress Catalog Card Number: 79-116553

Printed in the United States of America

To
Margaret Merry

Preface

Early childhood education is in a state of ferment today. The number and variety of innovative programs make it difficult for members of the profession to keep up with new developments. While some programs have been in existence long enough to be written up and others are in print before they have very much to report, a knowledge of still others can be gained only through site visits since little has been published about them.

A travel grant from the Carnegie Corporation of New York made it possible for me to make first-hand observations of innovative programs during a complete academic year. Project directors were most generous in making visits possible and supplying the theoretical backgrounds of their programs, but in some cases observation was necessarily limited for the sake of the personnel and children involved. In many ways the year's travel represents a survey of current developments.

The proliferation of innovative programs has its encouraging side; it signifies that education in the early years is being given the extensive thought and attention it requires. But this same proliferation makes it difficult to assess new directions and to put developments in perspective. During the year of my Carnegie Grant this need became so obvious to me that I was spurred to attempt not only to place new developments into a meaningful framework, but also to recommend changes for early childhood education obviously stemming from long-range perspectives.

With all early childhood educators I am glad to share insights that hopefully will extend their understanding of:

1. Developments in the field of early childhood education.

2. Current theoretical bases for programs.

3. Some of the constants that cannot be ignored when working with young children.

4. New directions required by society today.

While main sections of the book are devoted to descriptions of programs visited, these are preceded by a chapter on the theoretical trends which undergird early childhood education, both in the recent past and the present. A year of intensive observation and study could not help but provoke strong convictions about the directions early childhood education needs to take. These are presented in the final chapter. The directions are sketched in broad strokes, with details to be filled in according to the specifics of a particular situation, but in their significance they are universal.

Evelyn Weber

Acknowledgments

In writing a book of this nature an author is indebted to many sources. A special note of gratitude is in order to project directors who not only made site visits possible but gave permission to quote from unpublished materials so generously given to me. These projects include:

Parent Education Project — Ira Gordon
Frank Porter Graham Child Development Center — Halbert B. Robinson
Denver Public Schools — William R. Spears
Computer-Based Instruction — Richard C. Atkinson
The Children's Center — Bettye Caldwell and Julius Richmond
A Piaget-Derived Curriculum — Constance Kamii
Liverpool Laboratory School — William J. Meyer
University Elementary School, UCLA — Madeline Hunter
The New Nursery School — Glen Nimnicht
Nurseries in Cross-Cultural Education — Mary B. Lane
Cooperative Research Project, Tucson District No. 1 — Marie M. Hughes
Early Childhood Education Study — Allan Leitman
Study of Intellectual Stimulation of Disadvantaged Pre-Kindergarten Children — Helen F. Robison
Preschool Curriculum Demonstration Project — David P. Weikart
Stanford Program in Computer-Assisted Instruction — Patrick Suppes
Learning to Learn School — Herbert A. Sprigle
Bank Street Early Childhood Center — Elizabeth Gilkeson and Hy Wolotsky

For permission to quote from their publications I am grateful to the following publishers:

Harcourt, Brace and World, Inc.
Harper and Row Publishers, Inc.
Association for Supervision and Curriculum Development
National Association for the Education of Young Children
Association for Childhood Education International
Phi Delta Kappan
John Wiley and Sons, Inc.
Springer Publishing Co.
Teachers College Record
Rand McNally and Co.
Theory Into Practice
The Ronald Press
Basic Books, Inc.
Curriculum Laboratory, Goldsmiths' College, University of London
Teachers College Press

Contents

Early Childhood Education:
Perspectives on Change

1 General Trends in Early Childhood Education

At no level is educational ferment greater than in early childhood. Never has the education of the young child assumed greater importance in the eyes of the general public. Project Head Start and other programs for young children initiated by the Office of Economic Opportunity have put a measure of urgency upon the extension of educational opportunities for the very young. Legislation has set a timetable for establishing mandatory kindergarten programs as in Massachusetts and North Carolina. The Board of Regents of New York State in its momentous Position Paper of December 1967 has taken the lead in suggesting that all children benefit from education in the very early years(1). Thinking and learning, the board states, are enhanced by exposure to a wide variety of materials, equipment, and activities under the guidance of a competent teacher. It proposes that long-range planning in the state of New York include free public education for all three- and four-year-olds whose parents wish them to attend.

Beyond the desire for extending preschool education are the efforts to change the curriculum. There are projects throughout the country modifying or revolutionizing prekindergarten programs, with most such projects especially concerned with the economically disadvantaged child. They range from developmentally oriented programs, such as the Pre-Kindergarten Demonstration Center in Rochester, New York, to the highly demanding Bereiter-Engelmann program at the University of Illinois, cogently labeled a "pressure-cooker" approach(2).

Early Childhood Education Defined

For the purposes of this book the ages included in early childhood education will be broadly conceived. For some time educators in the field have considered the years from three to eight as developmentally and psychologically one—thus encompassing the years for nursery school, kindergarten, and the primary grades. The increased interest in infancy and the toddler years as an integral part of the intellectual growth cycle, as well as of other aspects of growth, expands the term to encompass all children under and including eight years of age. While in the literature there exists a lack of convention in the use of the term, it will be thus broadly used here.

General Trends

The surveyor of early childhood education today finds a number of readily identifiable trends. Groups of children tend to be smaller with more mixing of age levels. In some classrooms three- and four-year-olds are together and the group limited to around fifteen children. The adult-child ratio is changing with expanding use of teacher aides. Frequently, there are three adults in a classroom of fifteen children. Since curriculum revision is a concern of most project directors, there is a trend to reduce the number of hours children attend school and to leave built-in time for the staff to consider the kinds of experiences to be provided children. The significance of these organizational factors lies in what they make possible in curriculum reorganization and in authentic teacher-pupil relationships.

Another significant trend relates to efforts to reach the parents of young children and to involve parents in the educative process. Projects such as the Bank Street Early Childhood Center and Nurseries in Cross-Cultural Education in San Francisco work with parents in fundamental ways with the view that education must be geared to total needs. The emphasis is upon parent involvement in their child's education both at home and at school. It also includes helping parents become more adequately functioning members of society. This is far from parent education as formerly conceived and holds the promise of having a significant social impact.

Little change is evident in kindergarten per se. This seems to be the no-man's land of education today despite new legislation requiring kindergarten education for all children. It is still too early to evaluate the impact of Head Start on the kindergarten curriculum.

Innovation in primary education, as it belongs within the early childhood realm, relates to two major areas: one in school organization, the other in subject-matter fields. At the School of Inquiry in Rochester, New York or the University Elementary School at UCLA, for example, the organization of the school holds promise for providing for individual differences in children—a factor more frequently discussed than considered in school planning. At UCLA, multi-age groupings and team teaching focusing upon individual diagnosis and prescription for each child have broken the traditional age-grade, lock-step procedure effectively. At the School of Inquiry in Rochester, multi-age grouping coupled with interest centers strategically located throughout the school promise exciting individual and small-group experiences for children. This last school, incidentally, is located in a slum area of Rochester, but is a completely integrated school. White and black children from every suburb are enrolled, as well as children from the surrounding slum area. Some suburban parents actually regret that their child cannot attend this school situated in a run-down area—an interesting reversal of trends.

Other major changes in the primary grades are in the teaching of mathematics, reading, science, and social studies. Not many of these changes will be reported here. Indeed, they are so numerous that probably only one could be investigated in a year's time. Some mention, however, will be made of the work in elementary school science by Dr. Robert Karplus at the University of California in Berkeley. Karplus has worked closely with specialists in child development and has concentrated on the developmental theory of Jean Piaget. The science materials being designed at Berkeley hold interesting possibilities in the hands of a creative teacher.

Interest in the young child is not limited to children of nursery, kindergarten, and primary ages. There is a growing trend to extend the educational process to parents and infants. Efforts are being made to break the deprivation cycle by involving parents in the education of their infants and toddlers. One program of this nature is directed by Dr. Ira Gordon at the University of Florida. Trained, indigenous workers are going into homes to work with mothers of children as young as four months old. This particular project has had salutary effects upon the infants and mothers as well as upon the indigenous parent workers. Adults have assumed greater responsibility for children's learning; children have evidenced improved functioning in language, physical coordination, and social responsiveness.

Many projects involve cooperation between the education department of a university or college and the public schools of the area. While the public schools can provide the classroom organization in which new programs can be tried, the college faculty is largely responsible for innovative ideas and the theoretical framework which undergirds fresh ideas.

Fundamental Curriculum Change

While certain generalized trends in early childhood education can be readily identified, a discussion and assessment of fundamental program change is much more difficult; such change is imbedded in philosophic positions and values in addition to changing psychological beliefs.

Education in the preschool years has always been responsive to prevailing assumptions about the nature of man and his development, the ways in which learning takes place, and sociological concerns. The heightened concern for the nature of programs for young children follows a period of stability in early childhood education and minimal curricular change. It is comparable, however, to the upheaval that took place in the kindergarten curriculum at the turn of the century. The kindergarten was the notable program for young children then in existence. During the first quarter of the twentieth century, this program moved from a Froebelian inspired curriculum founded upon a philosophic idealism to one based upon the objective elements of science as applied to education(3). The change was slow and painful. One has only to read reports of the meetings of the International Kindergarten Union to find that a bitter pedagogical battle ensued in which leaders in the kindergarten movement became labeled "conservatives" or "progressives"(4). The progressive kindergarten leaders found a new theoretical framework to support a reconstructed curriculum in the philosophy of John Dewey, the child study of G. Stanley Hall, and the learning theory of Edward L. Thorndike(5). Changes in the kindergarten curriculum were deemed essential long before the new directions became clear. Dissatisfaction with established educational procedures became apparent three decades before new program strategies became clarified and put into practice. During an extensive period of trial and error, a more democratic classroom organization was developed in which children were given freedom of choice in activities. Completely different educative materials were created(6).

Later in this century, the impact of Arnold Gesell's views of human development was felt in kindergarten theory. The child was viewed largely in terms of the normative, overt behavioral data collected during this period. Nursery schools, developing a little later, incorporated the ideas of neo-Freudians as articulated by Lawrence

K. Frank and Daniel Prescott. Currently, a new emphasis placed upon the cognitive development of the young child is giving rise to new curricula. The theoretical base for these changes is found in the work of Jean Piaget explaining the development of intellectual structure, and in the writings of J. McVicker Hunt and Benjamin Bloom highlighting the importance of early environmental encounters for learning and stressing the significance of stimulation in the early years for later learning.

Early childhood education seems to be embarking on a period of trial and error in program change comparable to the one at the turn of the century. A survey of ongoing programs gives evidence that there is no consensus concerning the most relevant and fruitful educational experience for the child under six. Such programs embrace a wide range of objectives and diverse educational strategies. The very existence of such disparate early childhood centers reveals dissatisfaction with nursery education as it has developed from the 1920's. The student of program modification finds researchers making increasing use of the theories of a new group of psychologists—J. McVicker Hunt, Benjamin Bloom, and Jean Piaget. It is essential to probe the theoretical bases which undergird the existent diversity in curricula in order to understand them and to access their effectiveness. Since this is a transition period in early childhood education, the task of relating theory to practice is a difficult one. It is undertaken here with the hope of helping to clarify some obvious problems in the field today.

Reports of innovative projects in early childhood education follow the discussion of theoretical rationales. The programs described in this book are those which I visited during the academic year 1967–68 through a grant from the Carnegie Corporation of New York. These visits, illuminated by discussions with project directors and by what has been put into writing, were invaluable in my assessment of the new directions in early childhood education.

Notes

[1]Regents of the University of the State of New York, *Prekindergarten Education, A Position Paper* (Albany, New York: The State Education Department, December, 1967), pp. 5-12.

[2]Maya Pines, "A Pressure Cooker for Four-Year-Old Minds," *Harpers Magazine* (January, 1967), pp. 55-61.

[3]Patty Smith Hill, "Some Conservative and Progressive Phases of Kindergarten Education," in *The Kindergarten and Its Relation to Elemen-*

tary Education, Sixth Yearbook of the National Society for the Study of Education, Part II (Bloomington, Ill.: Public School Publishing Co., 1907), pp. 61-86. See also, Elizabeth Mechen Fuller, "Early Childhood Education," in *Encyclopedia of Educational Research,* ed. Chester W. Harris (New York: Macmillan, 1960), p. 390.

[4]Evelyn Weber, *The Kindergarten: Its Encounter with Educational Thought in America* (New York: Teachers College Press, 1969), pp. 65-72.

[5]*Ibid.,* pp. 48-55.

[6]Charlotte G. Garrison, *Permanent Play Materials for Children* (New York: Scribners, 1926).

Forces Propelling Change

The insights which brought about a revised curriculum for early childhood education by the 1920's were derived from philosophical, psychological, and societal forces. Pragmatism replaced an entrenched philosophical idealism; reliance upon scientifically derived data of human development supplanted faith in introspective analyses; a growing humanitarian concern for the poor impelled educators to look more carefully at the development of the young child(1). Let us turn briefly now to those insights that fostered a new curriculum based on principles which early childhood education relied upon until the 1960's. A brief examination of established convention will serve as a basis for estimating what is new in the educational scene on which a more stringent reconstruction of the curriculum can be based.

Philosophical Bases

The shift at the turn of the century from faith in a philosophical idealism to a pragmatic orientation was a revolutionary one shared not only by other levels of education but by all of society. Charles Darwin's *Origin of Species*, published in 1859, was the bombshell which influenced traditional outlooks on the world emphasizing "order, finality and comprehensiveness" and looking "upon truth as essentially fixed and permanent" to mold beliefs which "began to stress incompleteness, contingency, novelty, and change as real aspects of the world of nature and man and to look upon truth and knowledge as achievements of human experience"(2). For the pragmatist knowledge grew from human experience, ideas changed as a result of experience, and truth developed as a consequence of the testing of ideas(3). This represented a revolutionary reversal in philosophy with a sharp impact upon leaders in early childhood education whose program had been based upon the idealistic beliefs of Friedrich Froebel(4).

From Froebel's Idealism to Dewey's Pragmatism

John Dewey, whose influence was felt upon all educational levels, led early childhood educators into a new philosophical orientation when he wrote directly for them. In his functionalism he stressed the nature of the social interaction of individuals and their environments. He saw the individual as possessing dynamic qualities of interest and effort which were integral parts of the interaction. For work with young children, Dewey emphasized the enlarged part of social interaction as it contributed to democratic living: "The primary business of the school is to train children in cooperative and mutually helpful living; to foster in them the consciousness of interdependence; and to help them practically in making the adjustments that will carry this spirit into overt deeds"(5). Progressive early childhood leaders used the ideas of child interest, active interaction, and cooperative endeavors as key words in their curriculum design. This was the beginning of the elevation of the value of social cooperation among young children.

The break with philosophical idealism was sharp and profound. Dewey's writings provided clear directives for a revised educational program. In the writings of leaders such as Patty Smith Hill and Alice Temple, the effect of Dewey's thinking is evident. Especially in the early years of this century they looked to him for leadership. While Froebel had believed the joyous participation of children in the educational activities he devised would bring about a sense of social harmony, his program in America had become heavily teacher-directed with little chance for interaction among peers(6). The child in the American kindergarten sat quietly and manipulated objects as the teacher directed. The followers of Dewey introduced a work-play period in which social interaction was free and natural. The child in the Hill or Temple kindergarten actively chose materials and, perhaps, a small group of peers and worked with them guided by his own plans and ideas. Alice Temple recommended group projects holding meaning for the child and a wide variety of activities as a way of providing for individual initiative and cooperative endeavors. Social growth was expected to come through "practice of desirable social behavior" as children worked and played together(7).

Patty Smith Hill wrote of the reconstructed curriculum of the 1920's as one which served as a laboratory of democracy, for she considered "the wisely directed liberty" of the child as a "medium in which habits of self-direction and social cooperation could be established"(8). Miss Hill linked the social interactionism of Dewey to a concept of habit formation derived from psychology that eventually led to an elevation of designated habits as goals for the education of young children. She failed to realize that a fixed set of habits used as objectives tended to negate the flexible pragmatism Dewey espoused. However, free social interaction has remained as a part of preschool curricula. It serves as one example of program change stemming from newly acquired philosophical views.

Philosophy in Early Childhood Today

No such revolutionary change in educational philosophy is apparent today. Indeed, some people suspect that we have outrun our ideologies and therefore effect curriculum change in an ad hoc manner(9). D. Bruce Gardner gives top priority to the clarification of a philosophy for today when he writes, "One big general need for the future . . . is the emergence of a philosophical basis for preschool education (the *psychological* basis has become increasingly clear over the past decade, in part by the excellent contributions of such men as J. McV. Hunt . . ., but the philosophical basis remains elusive and vague)"(10). In the writings on early childhood education today one finds few philosophical references.

In a survey of current philosophical inquiry and what it offers the school, William K. Frankena concludes that it offers more about "what it is like to be clear and rigorous" than about what can be taken bodily into the classroom(11). Both recent movements in philosophy—analytical philosophy and existentialism—he criticizes for their avoidance of laying down normative premises for thought and action, which, in his opinion, would augment their usefulness (12).

If clear philosophical directions are not apparent, changes in values are. The existentialists present a group of dispositions to be fostered: authenticity, commitment, decision, autonomy, devotion—dispositions dealing with *modes* of behavior rather than its *content* (13). This points out an interesting distinction, for the habits regarded as goals in programs for young children have largely been those with behavioral content—cooperation, courtesy, promptness, orderliness(14). Yet the modal dispositions dominate educational discussions today.

Three Prevailing Values

Three basic modal values prevail in current educational literature—individuality, creativeness, and relevance. The historical emphasis in American ideology has been upon individual worth. Yet schooling has been in groups and normative in nature. An ASCD committee writes, "For a half-century or more we have been preoccupied with a conception of human adjustment or mental health stated as a function of the norm. Our standards of human adjustment have been primarily statistical, defined in terms of the famous bell-shaped curve. The well adjusted were those who clustered about the norm. . . . Nowhere has its effect been more marked than in our thinking about the goals of education"(15).

The normative age-grade standards of the elementary school were deplored by Daniel Prescott as "not effective in practice and often . . . detrimental to a child's learning and adjustment"(16). He discusses many ways in which the traditional graded structure runs counter to what we know about how children learn and develop. While the normative emphasis may not be so dominant in nursery education, it is in the kindergarten and primary grades.

Uniqueness. Today, however, we find a renewed affirmation of the uniqueness of individuals which extends to a consideration of the growth of the person. According to Ross Mooney, a deep stirring marks a profound change in the American dynamic, moving away from the concern of a young nation to evolve social institutions in which individuals were unwittingly instrumental, to a pendulum swing that puts persons first(17). James Macdonald writes about the person in the curriculum, as opposed to the psychological concept of individuals which tends to treat them as objects of study and control(18). Extensive discussions of personal growth probe the dynamics of becoming a "self-actualizing" or "fully-functioning" person(19).

Creativity. Coupled with the concern for helping man realize his fullest potential is the search for fostering creativity. Regard for the child's creativeness has long been part of early childhood education. Froebel's oft-repeated phrase, "creative self-activity," shows his regard for the child's reaching out(20). The creative arts have long been an important part of the curriculum in early childhood. But the concept of creativity has enlarged over the years. No longer is it thought of just in connection with the arts, but also as part of original thinking in science and technology, and, indeed, in all aspects of living.

The elevation of this value has motivated psychologists to search for the vicissitudes of creativity: the traits of the creative person or situation and the conditions which foster or impede its development. Studies are revealing important links between creativity and other intellectual functions. J. Richard Suchman finds important relationships between creative thinking and conceptual growth(21). E. Paul Torrance believes that it may ultimately be demonstrated that creative thinking is as important in the acquisition of knowledge as memory(22). This broadened scope of thinking about creativity makes it an integral part of the learning process.

Relevance. Relevance is a word used more in connection with the education of the college student than that of the very young child. Yet it is crucial that early school experiences be vital and meaningful for children. A child must perceive early that he is an individual who can learn and that his thoughts have significance. To provide less is to sacrifice his potential for learning at the source.

How can the young child's early encounters include an intense, personal involvement with the world of things and ideas that will insure against indifference and superficiality? By having an educational experience that is, in the words of Barbara Biber, "attuned to the ordinates of early childhood: sensory-perceptual-motor modes of relating to experience, establishment of meaning through self-reference and personal experience, rapidly shifting bases of idea structures from contextual simultaneity to cause-effect paradigms, and, most important of all, the pre-eminence of the subjective life, expressed in the child's satisfaction with phantasy as a mode of bringing coherence into the welter of fact and feeling that constitutes his experience"(23). Meaning for the young child increases as educators recognize his need to use the self as a nucleus around which concepts grow. This is the polar opposite of educational pedantry and mere verbalization.

A concern for personal self-fulfillment, the development of enhanced creative powers, and relevancy in education as it contributes to the first two dispositions are not as yet the universal goals of education. But they form the groundwork for a commitment to the ultimate progress of mankind. The increased educational literature about the growing self and the fostering of creativity reflect a search for understandings which will help us eventually to attain these goals.

Divergent Objectives

The values of early childhood educators are implicit in the nature of the program they provide for children. Nowhere is the diversity of philosophic bases more evident than in the scope and delineation of objectives, whether or not these objectives are made explicit by program designers. Some researchers, so imbued in societal concerns, seem to leave out of consideration the growing self of the learner—his individuality. The early kindergartens were so concerned with the socialization of the child within American democratic values that they elevated a single set of values, thus making of the kindergarten a "melting pot" of acculturation(24). Contemporary examples of the school as an acculturator include "the admonition to teach children 'standard' English and to eradicate the children's native dialect"(25). Such a program as the Early Childhood Project at the University of California at Los Angeles, directed by Carolyn Stern, comes under this designation(26).

Other programs, especially those of a compensatory nature, see the early years as a time for promoting cognitive growth so that children can later function more readily within the school system as it is today. Such an emphasis includes learning classroom behavior which will enable them to fit into the existing system and allow for its perpetuation. An emphasis on the school subjects which represent the focal concern of the school—reading, mathematics, science—accompanies the molding of social behavior. Affluent parents see these emphases necessary to prepare their child for college entrance and eventually to aid the child to enter a desirable vocation. Parents from economically disadvantaged neighborhoods see the cognitive and social molding as providing readiness to learn marketable skills. The Bereiter-Engelmann program at the University of Illinois is an example of cognitive and social molding to prepare the child to fit into the existent school system. Such programs tend to ignore those "ordinates of early childhood" designated by Barbara Biber(27) and run great risk of providing experiences so unattuned to the self of the young learner that they have little relevancy for him.

If early childhood education is ever to achieve the promise of those turning to it with great expectance, its objectives must go beyond societal pressures. We must devise and make possible "fulfillment" education in which the three values of self-actualization, creativity, and relevance are pertinent. Some current programs hold these values high; for example, Nurseries in Cross-Cultural Education in San Francisco, the Tucson Educational Model, and some Infant Schools in England.

The Impact of Child Psychology

In the psychological realm, a tremendous shift in points of view is underway. William Martin puts this shift in perspective when he writes that the scientific study of behavior with its external conditioning and the scientific study of personality with its concern for motivations have led to viewing the child in a "state of mindlessness"(28). We are now ready, Martin asserts, to view the child not only as a reactor and a purposer, but also as a knower. While the lines are never quite this clear, this statement sets up the emphasis given to old and new developments.

Child Development

Child study is a relatively new branch of the behavioral sciences —less than a century old. After 1889, when G. Stanley Hall became President of Clark University, a leading institution in the area of psychological research, he "played a seminal role in the fields of child development, child psychology, and psychoanalysis"(29). Clark University quickly became the headquarters for an expanded child study movement. A history of the summer sessions at Clark reveals such influential leaders as Anna Bryan, Patty Smith Hill and Frederick Burke in attendance(30).

Hall was influenced by Darwinism and applied evolutionary theory to psychology in his beliefs about recapitulation. This theory assumes that in the development of each individual organism there is reflected the evolution of the race. Hall saw this development as instinctual and as proceeding in a pattern of predetermined unfoldment(31). His was a psychology preoccupied with heredity, leading him into the previously neglected areas of instincts, feelings, and the unconscious. In emphasizing these, Hall "serves as a bridge in America from Darwin to Sigmund Freud"(32).

Hall also made use of the observational method of Darwin. He led progressive kindergarten leaders into the new methodology by providing them with observational techniques: questionnaires, anecdotal records, and the analysis of products. Indeed, some kindergarten teachers assisted Hall in the collection of data. *The Contents of Children's Minds*, Hall's first revolutionary publication, was a report and interpretation of data collected by kindergarten teachers in the Boston Public Schools(33).

Beginning with the thirties, the influence of Arnold Gesell has been powerful. Gesell, a student of G. Stanley Hall, followed the objective, scientific procedures for data collection established by Hall, but more than that, he subscribed to Hall's basic assumptions about genetically predetermined development. Gesell's major scientific effort related to the establishment of norms of behavior. He wrote of the Yale Clinic, "The major research is directed toward a normative charting of behavior development," with the direct purpose of developing "norms of growth"(34). Studies at the clinic placed age as the most important developmental dimension and described development as "a progressive morphogenesis of patterns of behavior"(35). Underlying this conception of growth was a faith in a more or less automatic unfoldment of behavior as a function of morphological development. This belief in a predetermined unfolding of behavioral patterns became known, through Gesell, as maturational theory.

Gesell considered maturation, the innate processes of growth, fundamental and powerful. To parents and teachers Gesell wrote, "The total ground plan is beyond your control. It is too complex and mysterious to be altogether entrusted to human hands. So Nature takes over most of the task, and simply invites your assistance"(36). This, of course, supported an essentially "hands off" attitude. It was frequently interpreted that anatomical structure must precede function. In other words, giving a child practice in a skill for which he was maturationally unready was useless, whether it was stair-climbing, cutting, or reading. The entire concept of readiness, so readily accepted and applied to early childhood education, stems from this reasoning and these basic assumptions.

Though Gesell, in his writings, did stress the importance of individual differences and suggested that the norms developed were intended only to illustrate the kinds of behavior which tend to occur at a specific age, the very organization of his work into "ages and stages" implied that maturation proceeds in an orderly, fixed rate so long as the metabolic requirements of the infant and child were met. Intellectual growth was subsumed under this dominating belief, giving indirect support to the notion of fixed intelligence already set in motion by the measurement movement. The testing movement, tied as it was to the work of Alfred Binet in France, came to America with people who believed in fixed intelligence(37). Faith in nature rather than nurture, seemed to dominate the thinking of J.

McKeen Cattell and Henry H. Goddard, two psychologists professionally concerned with establishing mental testing. Intelligence came to be considered as "inherited capacity" and, as such, essentially fixed and immutable.

Both the development of norms of behavior and the use of mental testing were suitable extensions of the efforts to build a "science of education." Data were based upon objective observation of overt behavior. An earlier deletion of the term "consciousness" as a useful psychological concept had turned study to what could be observed and measured in overt, behavioral manifestations. The emphasis was largely upon the quantitative and objective—motor performance, sensory capacity, language attainment—in a rather segmented or compartmentalized approach. Of five-year-olds these generalizations of observed behavior were written, "It is a here-and-now world. . . . His rapport with the environment is very personal. . . . His cooperative play is usually limited to a group of three; and is conducted with chief concern for his individual ends rather than the collective ends. . . . Five is a great talker"(38). From such data categorized thus by age, the characteristics and abilities of a specific age level were delineated; fives were expected to act in a "five way." Furthermore, the norms were often mistakenly equated with "normal" behavior. There seemed to be a scheme of orderly development and it was incumbent upon parents and teachers to patiently wait for this unfoldment.

No one asked the important question of the nature of the population utilized for the derivation of norms. The population of children studied at the Yale Clinic was of "high average or superior intelligence" and came from homes of "good or high socio-economic status"(39). Essentially, Gesell used children of adults in the academic community. The same was probably true of the many other child study institutes that grew as a part of other universities where the search for normative, descriptive data spread(40). The norms were attributed to a growth pattern so powerful that it negated varying environmental circumstances inherent in the lives of people at different socio-economic levels.

The normative approach to viewing development was put rapidly into use in early childhood literature. An "average" or "normal" child was presented to the teacher. In regard to the kindergarten child, for example, the following statements illustrate the manner in which normative data were translated for direct use in formulating programs: "The kindergarten child's interest span, though steadily lengthening, is still short"(41). "A hardy child, the kindergarten enrollee is constantly active"(42). "The child of this age is becoming more adept at using his hands, but he is not yet ready for the fine muscle coordination that writing requires"(43). Such statements tended to portray five-year-olds as a very homogeneous group. It also tended to imply that growth patterns were immutable.

Paralleling the scientific study of behavior was a movement trying to unravel the development of personality. Whereas behaviorism tended to make child study more scientific and more objective, Freudian psychoanalysts looked upon the individual as a battleground for conflicting urges that could be revealed only by introspective methods. A major emphasis was placed upon the motivations and drives stemming from the non-rational subconscious. To this deeply individual focus of Freud, neo-Freudians have added a concern for social interaction and have given "greater attention to the culture as a source of the dynamics and desires of behavior" (44). Psychologists became more and more aware that interactions in the early years are significant in the development of the individual's mechanisms of adjustment.

What seemed to emerge from early studies was the need for the young child to experience sympathetic understanding, patient support, and tenderness so that he could accept the process of socialization without becoming resentful, hostile, or overly aggressive. Guided with gentleness and wisdom, it was expected that the child would be free of the mechanisms of adjustment which foster aberrant behavior(45). One response to this was a move from repressive discipline to an extreme permissiveness. Another response was freeing the avenues of artistic expression from any adult dictation so that painting, dramatic play, creative rhythms, etc., could serve as a release for feelings. This, too, seemed to imply a "hands off" attitude.

These early efforts to learn more about the nature of development were the innovative studies of their period. They undoubtedly added significant information, although some of the right questions were never asked and basic assumptions not properly probed. Early childhood educators, maintaining an attitude of respect for children, were eager to utilize all the lessons learned from the study of children themselves, and based their curricula upon child development data. Probably, the normative data were most thoroughly applied at the kindergarten level and analytic psychology was most influential during the nursery school years.

Hall elevated the physical and emotional aspects of growth. His insistence that large-muscle development preceded the control of the finer muscles brought about a change in learning materials

(46). Many of the norms of growth presented by Gesell were physical and social in nature. What early childhood leaders acquired from Dewey related to the social organization of the classroom. Neo-Freudians added insights into emotional developments. Little wonder that in a preschool curriculum based upon knowledge of child psychology, the most enlightened developments have related to the physical, social, and emotional growth of the young child.

New Trends in Child Psychology

The scientific study of man placed stress on the overt performance of the individual. The psychoanalytic study of man placed stress upon adjustment. Both, in the opinion of William Martin, "rob the human being of the one characteristic that was once thought to be unique in man, that is, the fact that he has a mind and he has a capacity for thought"(47). But new developments are bringing us to a consideration of cognition. Among these are phenomenological methods in psychology, studies of the effects of early sensory deprivation on cognitive functioning, and, above all, a growing number of studies on children's thinking including the work of Jean Piaget. Though these influences have been developing for some period of time, their impact is only now in evidence. It has been accelerated through the writings of J. McVicker Hunt and Benjamin Bloom.

Cognitive Growth. Probing Gesell's assumptions about automatic unfolding, Hunt, in his powerfully documented book, *Intelligence and Experience*, argues for the significance of environmental encounters and their influence upon development. Reversing the belief that one can stand back and wait for development to take place, Hunt demonstrates that environment influences not only what development takes place, but when that development will occur. He discards the general notion that behavioral development is an automatic aspect of anatomic maturation in lieu of a transactional model of growth which emphasizes the modifiability of development by experience. This exceedingly important consideration, denying that development is fixed, Hunt extends to intelligence. New evidence from a variety of sources is forcing a recognition of the crucial role of life experience in the development of intelligence. While "the genes set limits on the individual's potential for intellectual development, . . . they do not guarantee that this potential will be achieved and they do not, therefore, fix the level of intelligence as it is commonly measured"(48). New evidence demands a study of the experiential side of the matter "where the genotype-environment interaction occurs." Hunt states, "It is relatively clear that experience, defined as the organism's encounters with his environment, is continually building into the developing human organism a hierarchy of operations for processing information and for coping with circumstances"(49). This conclusion is a direct result of his careful analysis of the work of Piaget and others.

For years Piaget's work has been disregarded in this country because his "methode clinique" did not engender much enthusiasm from psychologists engrossed in statistical methods, sampling, variables, and all the other aspects of scientific study. But increasingly, Piaget has gained recognition. Urie Bronfenbrenner identifies cognitive functioning as one of the major streams of study today and suggests that it stems from the work of Piaget(50).

For Piaget, intellectual growth is a developmental process involving two interactive functions between the individual and his environment: 1) inward integration or organization called assimilation and 2) outward adaptive coping called accommodation. Assimilation occurs whenever an organism utilizes something from the environment and incorporates it into generalized and repeatable behavior termed schemata. Accommodation operates as the environmental circumstances demand coping which modifies existing schemata. Thus, environment acts upon the learner not by evoking a fixed response or a passive submission, but by modifying existing schema. This dual process is the means whereby the reflexive responses of the newborn infant become progressively transformed through differentiations and coordination into logical organizations or operations for information processing. Development depends upon these two factors "equilibrating" each other through self-regulation. "Equilibration" is a process which Piaget considers pedagogically fundamental. It is a transitional mechanism continuously operating between the growing child and his environment. Furthermore, Piaget brings it close to individual development as he continually emphasizes self-regulation and self-correction(51).

The picture of the development of intelligence which emerges from the observations of Piaget and his collaborators is one of continuous transformations in the structure of logical thought. From birth to about eighteen to twenty-four months, the child is in the sensorimotor period of development when sensorimotor schemata are generalized and coordinated with each other and the child develops the beginnings of interiorized schemata. This is followed by an extensive period of concrete operations which has three phases: a preconceptual period to roughly four years of age, an intuitive phase which lasts until the child is about seven or eight years of age, and a third period of concrete operations(52). In the preconceptual and intuitive phases, the child makes "his first relatively unorganized and fumbling attempts to come to grips with the new and strange world of symbols"(53). The child's activity is dominated by symbolic play as he recollects actions (Piaget speaks of "interiorized images") and develops language. In the course of manipulation and social communication, the child extends, differentiates, and combines his action-images and simultaneously corrects his intuitive impressions of reality; i.e., space, causality, time. These preparatory periods come to fruition during the stage of concrete operations, roughly from the ages of seven to eleven, when "conceptual organization of the surrounding environment slowly takes on stability and coherence by virtue of the formation of a series of cognitive structures called groupings"(54). As the child repeatedly acts upon things and people, his thought becomes decentered from perception and action. Thus, it is only when the child enters the stage of formal operations at the age of about eleven or twelve that truly abstract thinking is possible so that logical deductions and generalizations can be made without reference to empirical evidence. The child becomes capable of extensions into time and space as his interactions with the environment build central processes which give him increasing autonomy and increasing dominance over perception and action.

Several important themes become clear through this picture of the epigenesis of the behavioral and thought structures comprising intelligence. First, though there is a gradual change, there are qualitative as well as quantitative changes in intellectual capacity; thus, there seem to be transition points in the process of continuous change. Second, only through continual and extensive interactions between the child and his environment does the child proceed to logical thought. Piaget makes it clear that direct experience, as well as social interaction with peers, are essential avenues for intellectual growth. Schemata develop through use, and the greater the variety of the situations to which the child must accommodate, the greater will be the foundations of logical thought. Further, through the processes of assimilation, accommodation, and equilibration, the individual plays an active role in his own intellectual growth. Self-regulation and self-correction are crucial; an active organism position is espoused.

Hunt speculates that learning centers upon the "problem of the match," between the inner integrative patterns a child has achieved and the external circumstances which will challenge him to accommodate without undue stress (55). When discrepancies are too large, they may constitute a source of distress or of negative motivation. When circumstances and central processes match perfectly, the result may be boredom and no development. The problem, then, is to find out how to govern the child's encounters with his environment so that accommodative modification will occur. Hunt believes that promoting this optimum rate of intellectual development would include self-directing interest and curiosity and genuine pleasure in intellectual activity. Furthermore, it would increase rather than decrease individual differences in intellectual capacity(56).

Thus, the total environment of the child takes on an educational aura, and a focus upon the environment is necessary to determine what responses are elicited and what behaviors shaped. The "problem of the match," however, places equal stress upon learner control of stimuli. The search must be for "the junction between the environmental press of stimuli and the inner integrative patterns of the individual"(57). Wide educational opportunities are opened up. But a danger is also possible through "forced closure for shaping when internal patterns are not 'matched' for this"(58).

Significance of Early Environment. In his book *Stability and Change in Human Characteristics*, Benjamin Bloom emphasizes the importance of the early years for intellectual development and the significance of environmental encounters in that development(59). In a masterful synthesis of existent research, Bloom concludes that "at least for extremes in environment there are clear-cut differences in the levels of intelligence reached by children"(60). And he hypothesizes that the effects of environment appear to be greatest in the early (and more rapid) periods of intellectual growth. Therefore, attention needs to be focused upon the enormous consequences of deprivation as it affects the development of general intelligence.

Bloom has not limited his study to intellectual growth, but has utilized research about other selected characteristics such as height, school achievement, interests, attitudes, and personality. With the exception of school achievement, Bloom found the most rapid period of development to be in the first five years of life. He expects that measurement instruments that are more precise will only demonstrate that he has underestimated the rapidity of early development. Following his thesis that characteristics are more amenable to change during the period of rapidly accelerating growth, Bloom hypothesizes that nursery school and kindergarten can profoundly affect "the child's general learning pattern"(61). Bloom's synthesis of research reveals the early years as significant for both intellectual and affective functioning. While his proposition that the early years hold great significance for personality development is in harmony with psychodynamic literature, his proposal that the early years are potent for intellectual growth is at variance with the tradition which put great faith in maturational theory.

Theory in Practice

One consequence of discounting the concept of unfolding is to raise questions about the role of maturation, with a host of concomitant questions concerning the timing of experiences. Alfred Baldwin concludes that "the concept of maturation seems to be an essential one some place in the theory of child development, although its exact role in a theory of behavior is by no means clear"(62). L. S. Vygotsky takes the position that intellectual structures are built through use, thus experiences should be aimed not so much at the ripe but at the ripening function(63). This presents a new concept which implies that readiness can be developed and that maturation plays a role in development but does not assure it. Theoretically, it implies a new sense of timing with many unresolved practical problems. How can we determine ripening functions? What experiences will enhance their development? Despite absence of substantive answers, it seems that some directors of early childhood programs are delving into the problem of the timing of experiences in preschool programs. In some instances they seem to be discarding not only the concept of a natural unfolding, but also the entire concept of maturation.

An experience I observed in Syracuse will serve to illustrate this point. A group of fifteen 3-year-olds were asked to find their place on a rug that had been taped into squares. In each square was a taped initial identifying the child's place. After finding their places, the children were asked to listen as a group to a recording of *Peter and the Wolf*. There was little evidence of comprehension or interest on the part of the children. After this listening experience these same children were given a choice of three activities: 1) stamping letters on paper, 2) using Montessori smell boxes, or 3) making a picture with melted crayons. These experiences imposed upon three-year-olds are part of the concern for timing. About this day care project for children considered deprived, Bettye Caldwell writes, "The project . . . represents an attempt to put to empirical test the general hypothesis that the timing of enrichment experiences may be as important as the nature of the experiences themselves"(64).

On another day I observed at the Liverpool Nursery School, directed out of the National Laboratory Center at Syracuse University, fifteen 4-year-olds asked to begin their school day by learning to tie shoelaces strung through a paper plate. Following this they could select their own activity. To those acquainted with the fact that girls come to school with different accomplishments than boys, including better fine muscle coordination, it will not be surprising that most of the girls quickly finished the task and went off to other activities. One girl learned to tie shoelaces that morning. With the joy children frequently experience in a new achievement, she repeated the act over and over again showing the bow to all observers. But for the boys it was different. Most of them struggled valiantly, but one boy threw the plate and laces to the floor in desperation. His frustration continued throughout the morning; the only thing he pursued at any length was throwing beanbags through a hole. When, at the end of the morning, he was asked to participate in a group using clock faces to tell time, he joined the group but refused to respond in any other way.

Taking seriously the evidence presented by Benjamin Bloom that the early years are potent for intellectual as well as for social and emotional development, large components of skill-learning tasks are being introduced to young children. In accepting J. McV. Hunt's repudiation of the reliance upon anatomic maturation as a means of selecting intellectual content, some people have forgotten that one of Hunt's major recommendations relates to what he calls "the problem of the match." The painful observational memories I have reported requires children to perform "mismatched" tasks. Hunt puts readiness (or the match) in Piagetian terms which state that learning takes place "when the child encounters circumstances which so match his already assimilated schemata that he is motivated by them but can cope with them"(65). Hunt further states that "on the side of practice, this notion of a proper match between circumstance and schema is what every teacher must grasp, perhaps only intuitively if he is to be effective"(66). If this reasoning is followed to its logical conclusion, it means that "the match" is an individual matter dependent upon intellectual schemata of the person. This compounds the already existent evidence of individuality in such elements as cognitive style, modes of thinking, and self-concept, and demands that we move toward more individual possibilities for learning.

An ad hoc pushing down of activities holding little meaning for these young children promises little for either enhanced functioning on their part or increased knowledge for the field of early childhood education. Instead of pushing experiences and materials for use at younger ages, radically different consciousness-expanding experiences seem called for. At this time, we need someone with the insight of a Froebel who can create new educational materials for young children as innovative for our time as Froebel's were for his.

Interactive Forces in Development

In order to provide truly enriching experiences the total growth of each child as a person must be considered. The complexity of behavior makes it difficult to deal with many aspects of development at once. For this reason we find projects investigating specific aspects and tending to ignore others. Some programs purporting to enhance the intellectual realm neglect the affective side of learning. One painful observation took place in Ypsilanti in a program designated as cognitively oriented. The group of three- and four-year-olds designated as deprived went to the grocery store to buy fruit to be used in a tasting experience the next day. On their return, however, the children were placed in groups of four or five with a teacher, and the grapefruit, oranges, apples, and bananas were used to talk about the quantitative terms of "more than" or "less than." The children's emotional investment in the fruit was not great so that interest and attention varied to the point where as an observer I questioned the actual "learning" of the terms, especially by one group of children. But when candy corn was used to extend the concepts, these economically deprived children were truly involved in the amount they received. Clearly, one little girl who had received only two pieces was painfully aware that she had less than the others, although she could not verbalize this fact to the satisfaction of the teacher. One small boy could not wait until after the discussion to taste the corn. He was frowned upon to the point where he continuously repeated, "I won't eat it again." The burden of guilt he developed far outweighed any cognitive learning that might have accrued. Cognitive and affective learning cannot be divorced. It is what is taking place in intact functioning of the child that is significant. Barbara Biber makes this clear when she writes, "Innovative thrusts, no matter how sound or imaginative each in its own way, are parts to be fitted into a conceptual whole, not for the sake of elegance of idea but because a classroom is a complex, human field of interacting forces and no part can have an insulated existence, theoretical or practical. Most significant for this task is the knowledge of human behavior available through advances made by developmental theorists in the analysis of cognitive processes, the growing interest in ego-development among psychoanalysts, the wealth of studies of the creative process and the recognition of the self as a psychic dynamism"(67).

Although the influence of Piaget, Hunt, and Bloom have been singled out here because they are used within the rationales of many new proposals and programs, other new theoretical directions are emerging. Harold Stevenson has written that "the last decade has been one of the most exciting and productive in the history of child psychology"(68). Among new developments, Boyd McCandless lists a renewed and imaginative approach to cognitive development, more attention to curiosity in the life of the child, investigations of creativity, experimental research into the affects of methods of child control, more increasingly sophisticated investigations of sex-typing and identification, refinement of Guilford's theory of the structure of the intellect, and imaginative research on the relations between body build and social adjustment (69). To translate new developmental understandings into school practice is difficult—especially since a synthesis of new understandings is requisite. But in no other way can their meaning for the total development of the individual be realized.

Theories of Learning

Only when the early childhood educators of the early 1900's added a new conception of learning to their changed beliefs about human growth were they able to present a new curriculum in written form for all to use. An analysis of *A Conduct Curriculum for the Kindergarten and First Grade*(70) reveals Edward L. Thorndike's stimulus-response psychology as a guiding force(71). In this book the desired outcomes of the program were listed in conjunction with what were considered to be appropriate stimulus situations. While flexibility was allowed and children were given considerable freedom and choice, nevertheless, the curriculum was presented in behaviorist terms. The book was developed in the 1920's under the direction of Patty Smith Hill at Teachers College, Columbia University where Thorndike was a co-worker.

A Science of Education

Thorndike had unbounded faith in the scientific method and its application to educational problems. With the goal of building a comprehensive science of education, he began with the improvement of educational method through scientific study and came ultimately "to the conviction that the aims, too, might well be scientifically determined"(72). It is easy to see why he arrived at this conclusion, since his methodology was only possible when goals—or desired responses—were worked out in minute detail. Such goals rest on an assumption of determinism with the designer of the curriculum the outliner of all that is important to know. While many consistently disputed this means for the derivation of goals, Thorndike's methodology influenced all of American education.

Learning, in Thorndike's opinion, was highly specific and consisted of the establishment of particular bonds of connection between a stimulus, S, and a response, R. Thorndike's famous laws of learning for the establishment of these bonds were known to a generation of teachers. He proclaimed the need to exercise and reward desirable connections and to prevent or punish undesirable ones(73).

Thorndike's laws emerged from the scientific laboratory. Before the turn of the century he inaugurated the laboratory study of animal learning and later went on to apply the knowledge gained to the general problems of psychology. Such application was based upon a revolutionary assumption which "represents a synthesis of scientific method and evolutionary doctrine, since in the absence of the latter animal learning would hardly have been considered a suitable topic for a psychologist"(74). He offered the results of his experimental efforts to teachers as a means of making education more efficient and effective.

Behaviorism was born in the early decades of this century from an amalgamation of Thorndike's associationism and the conditioning technique of Ivan Pavlov(75). John B. Watson published his book *Behavior* in 1914 and became the name associated with the term(76). He began his work with infants and young children. Openly repudiating introspection as a method of scientific study and turning to objectively observable behavior, Watson made possible the study of the very young. He was interested in emotional responses in infancy but eventually extended the use of conditioning beyond the realm of emotions to include all learning. Habits, attitudes, and the most complicated processes of thinking Watson postulated as built by the process of conditioning, whereby untold numbers of new and complicated stimuli were associated with a few innate reflexes.

In this picture of learning "the brain was conceived to be analagous to a telephone switchboard"(77). Learning consisted of impressions of new reaction patterns on a pliable, passive organism. Drill and repetition were considered useful devices for promoting the system of reflex arcs. Little attention was given to student purpose. Interests, understanding, and the relevancy of materials were subservient to the presentation of stimuli for the conditioning process.

Extensions of stimulus-response, conditioning theory are in vogue today and evident in some early education projects. They are known now as reinforcement theory or operant conditioning. The main teaching emphasis is upon the successive, systematic changing of the learners environment to increase the probability of desired operants or responses(78). This is another link in the chain of the scientific study of behavior. For neobehaviorists, followers of this learning theory, "operant conditioning is the learning process whereby a response is made more probable or more frequent; an operant is strengthened—reinforced. . . . In operant conditioning, teachers are considered architects and builders of students' behavior. Learning objectives are divided into a large number of very small tasks and reinforced one by one. Operants—sets of acts—are reinforced—strengthened—so as to increase the probability of their recurrence in the future"(79).

Reinforcement plays a large role in the thinking of some neobehaviorists, for this is the way they consider the repetition of new responses to be assured. Of course, reward and punishment have long been part of classroom learning situations. Teachers have traditionally used social reinforcement—praise, blame, smiles, frowns—to promote learning. Searching for a more reliable model of the learning process, contemporary S-R psychologists have dropped the terms "reward" and "punishment" in favor of "positive and negative reinforcement." Emphasis is on reinforcing agents—crackers, M & M's, small toys—whatever assures that the new operants will be repeated. The stimulus which produced the response in the first place is not the significant aspect in operant conditioning. Some—any—stimulus must elicit the desired response for operant conditioning to function, but the reinforcing agents, not the original causative factors, are the prime consideration(80).

This process is well illustrated by an arithmetic "lesson" where five-year-olds were being drilled on number recognition at the University of Illinois. The teacher wrote a number under ten on the chalkboard with instruction to the children to say the number before she did. The teacher kept a tally of the results. When a child said the number first he was given a cracker. Later when they moved on to simple addition there was a revealing exchange between the teacher and one child. The teacher gave them the problem of $3 + 4 = \square$, with the box in place of the answer. She was trying to establish the point that the box did not stand for a specific quantity. But to one young boy, □ dog was just as meaningful as three dogs or four dogs. The teacher finally got him to say that □ dogs did not stand for a numeric quantity, and he received a cracker, but there was no evidence of lasting comprehension. All of this was done at a verbal level; there was no recourse to counting objects or even drawings on the chalkboard. When the children were given a mimeographed page to complete, one boy said very quietly, "I have a headache." The teacher's response went something like this: "You're not thinking. That's why your head aches. If you think, you can do these problems. Then your head will not ache."

Donald Snygg has written that this shift in emphasis upon the reinforcer rather than upon the nature of the stimulus is a significant one, for there tends to be a vaguer relationship between the reinforcement and what is to be learned(81). "Reinforcement" is identified only by its consequences and gives the teacher little aid in planning. But the use of reinforcement, particularly primary reinforcement—the satisfaction of a basic biological need or drive—is evident in a number of preschool programs I visited. In the program described previously, this took the form of crackers. In other programs M & M candies are used. Still other projects for young children talk about "token economies." This means giving children tokens for approved responses which they can cash in for some trinket to take home.

As a total learning theory, operant conditioning, dependent as it is upon the key words "operants" and "reinforcement" can be accepted only by those who are willing to view the learner as passive and non-purposive and who tolerate the assumption of determinism. Turning first to the non-assertive role of the learner, in the classroom described the child was viewed as a disengaged intellect, divorced from affective and social realms. Not even the one child's softly murmured, "I have a headache," was recognized. Bigge and Hunt write, "Thorndike tried to be highly mechanical, but the neobehaviorists have developed psychological theories which are even more consistently mechanical than were Thorndike's"(82). This mechanical approach leaves no place for feelings, sensitivities, creativity, or a sense of autonomy in learning.

As for the assumption of determinism, the designer of this kind of curriculum does indeed become the outliner of all that is important to learn. Such determinism serves "to teach what is already known, to promote conventional conforming behavior, to prepare pupils to live in a world exactly like the one in which they are educated"(83). Donald Snygg has forcefully stated, "If what is desired is a creative, adaptable citizen, able to deal with problems his teachers could not have envisaged and with problems they were unable to solve, another model for learning must be used"(84).

Cognitive Field Theory

The other model Snygg refers to lies within the realm of cognitive field theory, the second major position of contemporary learning theory. These two dominant theories—conditioning theories of the stimulus-response, reinforcement family and the cognitive theories of the Gestalt-field family—should be thought of as large groupings, for proponents within each differ on many points. Yet the neobehaviorists hold certain key ideas in common, just as do the cognitive field psychologists.

Ernest Hilgard describes Gestalt psychology, the initial field theory, as coming in the late 1920's and 1930's "like a breath of fresh air upon the American scene, then dominated by a somewhat strident behaviorism"(85). Field theory has been influenced by the work on insight by Wolfgang Kohler(86), productive thinking by Max Wertheimer(87), cognitive structure by Edward Tolman(88), and others. Finding phenomenology hard to fit into the canons of quantitative science, researchers have not used it extensively as a framework for experimentation.

In cognitive field theory, learning phenomena are considered to be closely related to perception. "Consequently, learning (is defined) in terms of reorganization of the learner's perceptual or psychological world— his field"(89). Learning in this view is a nonmechanical development; it is instead a change of perception—or a modification of the person's life space. Life space contains the person himself and the total physical and psychological world in which an individual lives at a given point in time. Learning thus must be a relativistic process in which an individual modifies old insights or cognitive structures or develops new ones. Learning is a dynamic process of interactive experience whereby life spaces are changed to become more serviceable to the individual. In this process the learner is a purposive, exploratory, imaginative individual. Learning is facilitated by the discovery of personal meaning.

The field approach as a conceptual model for education, is exemplified, at least to a degree, in some nursery-kindergarten settings. I visited one nursery school which I believe comes close to this, for in it learning relates to the perceptual framework of the learners and is a dynamic process whereby, through interactive experience, the life spaces of the individuals are changed to become more serviceable for them. Picture a nursery school setting rich in materials and equipment to promote first-hand conceptual growth and to provide many kinds of environmental encounters for children. As I walked into the classroom, I found children either individually or in small groups engaged in a variety of experiences.

Three children were making strange creations out of combinations of wood and styrofoam. One girl was painting at an easel. Three others were involved in dramatic play in the housekeeping area. One small girl was striking letters on a typewriter made available to her. She asked what the letters said and then requested a teacher to type her name for her, which she repeated by herself.

A larger group of children were gathered around a table with a young male teacher. They were adding food coloring to water to observe the effect it had. The day before, they had tasted water, then added salt and sugar to taste the changes. In the process they enjoyed large amounts of sugar water! On the day of my visit, there were numerous small jars and cups with water into which they could drop the pure food colors. Some tasted the water and many soon began to mix colors and observe the effect. All this time there was a continuous flow of language. One child counted the drops of food coloring as she put them in the cups. Discussion of colors and changing colors spontaneously followed. One little girl brought cups and jars to me to show and explain the changes. Two children discovered that if they moved the jars of colored water into the sunlight the colors were more brilliant. Of their own volition, many of the children stayed with this experience a full twenty to thirty minutes.

The group I am describing was in San Francisco in one of the nursery school centers directed by Dr. Mary Lane. She calls them Nurseries in Cross-Cultural Education. There was a mixture of black, white, and oriental children, with a third of them coming from middle-class families and the other two-thirds from economically deprived families. This group had been together the previous year and the social and verbal interaction was extensive.

In what ways do these experiences fit the cognitive field theory of learning? These children were actively involved with understanding their world. They were deeply engaged in information processing. Their perceptions and the resultant concepts were embedded in realities of sight, taste, and touch as they encountered them as individuals. Further, the objective outcomes of learning numbers, colors, and transformations were mixed with the affective processes —the children's utter delight in their discoveries, the freedom and relaxation felt in "playing around" with challenging materials. They were learning, at their level, to explore and ask questions about the effect of sun on color, for example. Learning was a process of exploration and experimentation, through which the child could (and did) reach out toward a structuring of ideas which made sense to him.

Comparing Effects

In the preschool situation where children were being drilled in recognition of numbers and number facts, the children were forced to accept an adult structure of ideas no matter what meaning this had for them. In the second situation, children were allowed to structure meaning in a self-organizing, integrating process. Each child was developing a degree of autonomy in learning. Barbara Biber writes, "Teaching that enacts this line of thinking is expected to produce in children special cognitive skills assumed to be more flexible and successful as tools for intellectual activity than the kind of thinking styles learned by children who are made the passive recipients of didactic teaching. Further, the pleasure derived from fulfilling curiosity through a style of learning that encourages children to try out their capacities becomes its own reward and generates the motivation to keep on learning. Nor should we neglect the special dimension of self-feeling associated with these learning activities, the awareness of being the discoverer, the explorer of the unknown"(90).

In the first preschool classroom, an adult-systematized order was imposed upon children regardless of their ability to utilize it. The process was one of direct, verbal input. In the second situation, children were engaged in the mutual interaction of perceiving the environment and acting in it. They not only perceived the environment, but processed the information of what happened as they behaved. Of these two different kinds of experiences Ira Gordon writes, "Schooling which utilizes the child's endeavors to structure his world contributes to competence. Schooling which either tries to impose an order when the child cannot grasp it, or presents masses of data expecting the child to order them as the adult does, may lead to mental indigestion and feelings of incompetence"(91).

Henry Lindgren proposes that field theories appear to explain a great deal more of what we recognize as learning than do theories of the reinforcement type. "The latter," he states, "appear to be formulations of very specific types of behavior, particularly behavior that has some physiological or kinesthetic component. . . . Field theory . . . appears to embrace a much larger range of learning, particularly the learning involved in problem solving"(92).

All the implications of cognitive field theory for educational practice are not clear. But certainly it demands that meaning, individualization, readiness, "the match" be aspects of all learning situations. These can only be attained when the classroom organization is flexible enough to permit personal involvement on the part of all learners. It is ironical that today in a few innovative primary programs, schools are moving in the direction of greater flexibility and individualization while preschool classrooms are losing these qualities. In such schools as Nova School in Fort Lauderdale, Florida, The School of Inquiry in Rochester, New York, and some Infant Schools in England, new educational practice is emerging. Active involvement on the part of children is made possible. We cannot teach in one fashion and expect children to operate in another fashion. What is done in the early, formative years of development toward autonomy or passivity in the learning situation is undoubtedly particularly significant for later behavior. If educational goals include assisting individuals to become fully functioning persons, persons who can solve some of the world's perplexing problems, these seem more readily met when a cognitive field theory forms the basis for classroom experiences—at least when it dominates the educational scene.

We probably should not be asking the question, "Which theory of learning?" but rather, "What type of learning, under what conditions, for what educational goals?" Numerous life responses are and should be conditioned responses. If we had to think of each act in a new way each time—brushing our teeth, crossing a street, driving a car—it would be tedious indeed. In school, certain skill acquisitions demand eventual mastery through conditioned responses. In Palo Alto, I saw a computerized drill and practice session in arithmetic for children at about the fourth-grade level. The practice exercises these children were getting were tied to the work going on in their regular classroom. For about seven or eight minutes a day, on a machine similar to a teletype machine, the children had a practice lesson to help establish the automatic response of certain computational skills. The drill for each child was dependent upon the child's level of achievement as determined by a pre-test given that particular week. This operation made sense. Through feedback by the machine, correct answers were assured. The children were involved and responsible. It eliminated much boring work for the learner and the teacher. But notice the small amount of time given to this experience—seven to eight minutes a day!

Behavior Modification

Hunt talks about stimulus-response methodology as distinguished from stimulus-response theory and discusses conceptualized processes intervening between stimulus and response(93). Some researchers consider this methodology as a means of behavior modification in the social domain. Donald Baer and Montrose Wolf contend that in preschools, where the effect of the teacher's response to behavior is potent, it is important that the reinforcement contingency be recognized and deliberately planned(94). They found that the usual social reinforcement given by teachers, family, and peers which is effective for the middle-class child does not operate with the economically deprived child. They comment that "a stimulus should be found for that contingency which does indeed function as a reinforcer; if that stimulus cannot be a social one, then a more tangible substitute—a difference in detail, after all—can be found"(95).

The treatment of Lisa, at the age of three years and three months in a cooperative nursery school, will serve as an example of behavior modification(96). The child's activities in the classroom were "hyperactive, disruptive and difficult to control." They included screaming and throwing things, biting, hitting, grabbing, pushing, and not responding to instructions. The treatment included removing the child from the classroom following disruptive behavior, reinforcing socially acceptable behavior by teacher praise and attention, and some ignoring of inappropriate behavior. Over a period of time observational data reveal disruptive behavior significantly reduced. Such research is certainly revealing to teachers who tend to give a great deal of attention to disruptive behavior, thereby reinforcing it.

Even a limited amount of behavior modification of the sort described is unacceptable to those convinced that the psychodynamics of growth are more complex and who repudiate the assumption of a passive, non-purposive child. The demand for conscious molding on the part of the teacher is hard to reconcile with the lack of imputing conscious behavior on the part of the child. With the assumptions forming the basis of each family of learning theory so at odds, it is difficult to see how a synthesis can be worked out or how stimulus-response methodology can fit into a cognitive field theory.

Research on the Conditions of Learning

Rather than efforts at synthesis, other study is focused upon enlarging our understandings of the nature and conditions of learning. For example, through factor analysis, J. P. Guilford has detected five major groups of intellectual abilities classified according to operations: cognition, memory, convergent thinking, divergent thinking, and evaluation(97). His analysis also classifies factors according to the kind of intellectual content involved: figural, symbolic, semantic, behavioral, and according to products: units, classes, relations, systems, transformations, implications. Such a system might serve as a useful basis for considering the curriculum for young children. In some curricula, memory, convergent thinking, and symbolic content may prevail at the expense of other factors.

The research on the vicissitudes of creativity exposes conceptions of a preschool program that lie dormant. For despite consistent emphasis on the creative arts in programs for young children, I found little effort to utilize the increasing knowledge about conditions which hinder or foster creative thinking. The following characteristics have been identified by E. Paul Torrance as playing some role in the creative process: verbal fluency, non-verbal fluency, originality, inventiveness, constructiveness, elaboration, curiosity, and hypothesis formation(98). Three conditions within an individual which are closely associated with a constructive, creative act are defined by Carl Rogers: openness to experience, maintaining an internal locus of evaluation, and the ability to toy with elements and concepts(99).

While at least one psychologist, David Ausubel, still prefers to think of creativity as a particularized capacity, normally distributed in the population(100), many others are taking the broadened view of developing the creative potential of every child and designating this as one of the functions of the school. Research on conditions which give us new ways of conceiving the elements in the educational environment may, at this time, be more helpful to the teacher than one carefully formulated theory of learning. This may be especially true of the education for very young children, because many of the conditions necessary for creative endeavor form a fundamental part of their developmental characteristics—characteristics such as openness to experience, freedom to experiment, spontaneous flexibility, and, of course, curiosity. The sometimes almost unbearable curiosity of the young child is recognized by those in association with him. He explores, he manipulates, he questions, he wanders, he interrupts in satisfying this driving force within him.

The responses made to the young child's early expressions of curiosity may have long-lasting effects and set the pattern for his total subsequent explorations. We know that this driving force, the opposite of passivity, can be readily stultified and lost as a propulsion to learning. Or continual long-winded answers on the part of adults may have the effect of making the child overly dependent upon the adult and of building a regard for the adult as the receptacle of knowledge from which information is obtained. The ready answer tends to terminate questioning and exploration, while instead, a questioning technique may lead the child as young as nursery school age into the inquiry process(101). Such questioning can provide clues which enable the child to seek his own answer. The maximum use of the child's impulse to be curious may include his being able to obtain and integrate information from varied sources.

One central task of early education may be to keep the creative potential alive for learning. This undoubtedly means allowing and supporting the young child's inventiveness in language, construction, dramatic play, and fantasy.

Transactional Model Man

Putting together a concept of learning which views man as a purposive, exploratory individual and new conceptions of human development which emphasizes intelligence as modifiable, the importance of environmental transactions, and the individual as an active, self-organizing system, Ira Gordon gives us a new model to depict changing beliefs(102):

Linear Causation Model Man	*Transactional Model Man*
A mechanistic, fixed closed system characterized by	An open-energy, self-organizing system characterized by
1. development as orderly unfolding	1. development as modifiable in both rate and sequence
a. physical-physiological-genetic	a. genetic-experiential
b. socio-emotional: antecedent-consequent	b. socio-emotional: field, transactional
c. intellectual-fixed	c. intellectual modifiable
2. potential as fixed, although indeterminable	2. potential as creatable through transactions with environment
3. a telephone switchboard brain	3. a computer brain

Linear Causation Model Man	*Transactional Model Man*
4. steam engine driven motor	4. a nuclear power plant energy system
5. inactivity until engine is stoked	5. continuous internal flow of activity
6. additive collection of past	6. organization into a system
7. uniqueness essentially genetic.	7. uniqueness continuously evolving from organism-environment transactions.

Gordon proposes these terms only as metaphors, but they clearly point up changing views. He also points to the lag between emerging ideas and their acceptance by educators who have formed their behavioral concepts in the "linear causation" world. Not only does this model encapsulate changing conceptions, but it can be used to point up discrepancies in developing programs. For while some programs have discarded the belief in orderly unfolding, they still insist upon the "telephone-switchboard" view of learning, thus mixing models in an unfruitful manner. A consideration of this model will be helpful as we begin to look at specific innovative programs.

The transactional model clearly depicts the child as an information-processor resulting from his organism-environment encounters. The continuous flow of activity explains the active, curious, inquiring, poking, seeking activity of young children. Most significantly it explains the uniqueness of individuals as continually evolving from organism-environment transactions. In other words, growth and learning depend upon internal factors such as maturation, and external factors both physical and social coming together in a personal way. Uniqueness and individuality permeate each organism-environment encounter. Individuality, then, is a constant emergent.

Programs that build conformity of activity and expression may cut persons off from their own creative selves. Even as we endeavor to shape children's behavior, Macdonald recommends a flexible, multi-dimensional program with constant possibilities for child choice. "What is often called play," he writes, "will be a major avenue of growth, although what is 'played with' will undoubtedly be continually improved as our understanding grows of the manner in which concepts are embodied in things"(103). Play, in which the child experiences autonomous encounters with the environment, is a part of learning in the transactional model.

The Sociological Impact

The critical nature of our times has brought into focus the problems of the poor. Society has turned to education, as well as to economics, as a means of alleviating these problems. Educationally, it becomes increasingly important to look back into the roots of problems—into the beginnings of learning in school and in the home. Therefore, we find an unprecedented focus upon the infant and the young child.

Education for a Better Society

Significantly heightened interest in early childhood education has frequently accompanied a widespread concern for society in general or for a special segment of society. When Plato contemplated the educational plan for people in his ideal Greek society, he included a program for the years under six. He wrote that "the beginning is the most important part of any work, especially in the case of a young and tender thing, for that is the time at which the character is being formed and the desired impression is most readily taken"(104). He suggested the early years as critical for developing not only the child's body and healthy habits, but also for fostering good breeding through sports, games, plays, and songs. Music, in the Greek sense, was a most important nourishment for the young as it was inseparable from harmony. Plato expected that during the early years education could lay the foundation for wisdom, temperance, courage, and justice—the four cardinal virtues of the perfect citizen of the Republic.

Through the ages, curricula can be linked to a continual concern for social betterment. The conception of education held by both Jean Jacques Rousseau and Johann Pestalozzi included the development of the powers of the individual. They both viewed human nature as innately good; the enhancement of individual powers meant progress toward an improved society. To maximize the goodness of persons for an improved society, the early years needed conscious attention. For Pestalozzi, this meant loving care from others—especially the mother—from the earliest stages of life(105). For Rousseau, it meant guarding the child from the vices of society and emancipating him from unintelligent and cramping traditions(106).

The educational plans of Froebel, that unique organizer of early childhood education, had enlarged social connotations. Froebel lived in Germany during the period of the Napoleonic wars. In their destructive influence, he not only saw childhood imperiled but also felt the breach war engendered in the unity of all living things. This lack of social unity was to Froebel a major threat to mankind's struggle for a better life. Only in a loving community of men did Froebel believe the child could be helped to ascend to the understanding of the metaphysical unity of the universe, the outstanding component in Froebel's view of life(107). Hence, his demand for a cooperative rather than a competitive classroom situation and his insistance that social values would accrue from many of the "plays" of childhood. Of play he wrote, "The plays of childhood are the germinal leaves of all later life, for the whole man is developed and shown in these, in his tenderest dispositions, in his innermost tendencies"(108).

Social and Emotional Adjustment

When the kindergarten came to the United States, its rapid expansion was linked to social reform. While some of the first kindergartens were private enterprises for children of wealthy parents, many more developed as centers for providing benevolent nurture for the children of the poor(109). The rapid extension of kindergarten in the United States came during the 1880's and 1890's and was interwoven with the settlement movement. Indeed, some settlements started with the establishment of a free kindergarten for the children of immigrants drawn to our large cities by growing industrialization(110). The "free kindergarten association" usually developed under the aegis of a group of lay people with philanthropic interests who searched then for a professionally trained teacher to work with the children. Thus, in the early years of expansion, the kindergarten was supported by a community of laymen in close contact with professionals. The prime purpose was starting the young child on the "correct" path in life and thereby ultimately improving society. These free kindergartens, socially impelled, formed the nucleus for public school kindergartens, for many of them were assimilated into public school systems.

Kindergarten in the early years was not looked upon as hastening the child's entrance into traditional primary education. Instead, kindergarten was considered of great value in fostering the moral and spiritual growth of the young child at a most malleable period of development. Elizabeth Peabody, a leader in the kindergarten movement, straightforwardly proclaimed moral education to be "the Alpha and Omega of the kindergarten"(111).

When faith in the philosophy of idealism, which formed the basis for Froebel's program, waned, the long, slow reconstruction of the curriculum began. Faith in the social and moral value of kindergarten continued, however, in full force. Those ardent leaders responsible for the revised kindergarten program, especially Patty Smith Hill and Alice Temple, had experienced the concern for social reform that had dominated the earlier period. They did not abandon this objective, but in general their faith in social reformism was now evidenced in the projected plan for habit formation in the young. The *Conduct Curriculum* came forth with its parallel listings of activities and the hoped for "changes in thought, feeling, and conduct"(112). By uniting desired outcomes with appropriate stimulus situations, the writers believed they were providing effective practice for the enforcement "of changed behavior due to a changed nervous system." In Miss Hill's words such a curriculum was expected to "lead to habits of behavior, finally culminating in character"(113). Illustrative behaviors include such abilities as sharing materials, learning to play cooperatively, respecting the ideas of other children, and developing a sense of responsibility. Obviously, these goals were part of the middle-class values of the teachers who helped compile the list. The emphasis was decidedly upon social and moral behavior.

The nursery school movement which emerged in England reflected the psychoanalysis of Sigmund Freud(114). Writers in the field of nursery school soon began to talk about freeing the child from over-repressive discipline so that natural impulses would not be driven below the threshold of consciousness and leave dangerous residues. The belief that behavior is caused gained credence as nursery school teachers were admonished to study the underlying causes of behavior. A new reason for play was recognized; it was considered the medium for the child's revelation of his inner feelings(115). The psychoanalytic belief in the tremendous importance of infancy and early childhood for emotional growth supported the efforts to promote education at this level. Thus, in the nursery school, the development of emotionally stable individuals was a major goal.

The normative data of the 1930's so readily used in early childhood education to present an average or "normal" child pictured the kindergarten child as having a short attention span, good large-muscle coordination but little control of the finer muscles, a vocabulary size of two thousand words, and so forth. The implication of this presentation of normative data was always that the program be built around the nature and characteristics of children. For example, in consideration of his short attention span, the child should have only short periods of concentrated work; he should be protected from fatigue by frequent rest periods. The regard for the nature of the child became known as the child development point of view(116). The curriculum based upon this view might be termed a "needs" curriculum in a developmental sense. In the literature many physical, social, and emotional needs are defined, but little in the intellectual realm beyond the "need to know."

Thus, until the decade of the 1960's, early childhood education has been conceived as contributing to society by helping young children become more effective individuals through "character training" or "social and emotional adjustment." Too often the process has been one of molding the young child to a middle-class code of ethics. But many programs are now utilizing revised conceptions of the psychodynamics of growth for both individuals and social reasons as we shall see in some programs to be described.

Intellectual Competence

Today, early childhood education is being challenged to make its contribution to a great society in a way never before contemplated. The focus has swung to the cognitive growth of the very young. Many programs seem only to be aiming at a "cognitive tooling up" of the very young child so that he can "make it" in an established school situation. Other programs are aspiring to fit new knowledge of cognitive growth into a larger framework of human development. However the change is viewed, it is always tied to the crumbling concept of fixed intelligence. So long as it was believed that intelligence was genetically determined, the inferiority of children who tested below normal on standardized intelligence tests was wrongly accepted. With the recognition that something could be done about a youngster's intelligence by the nature of the kinds of experiences provided him, new hope has impelled a search for the "appropriate" and "optimal" stimuli which will enable the child with meager background to function more adequately intellectually. At this point, we do not know what constitutes either appropriate or optimum stimuli. But the search is on. Faith in nurture rests upon a "transactional" view of learning and development, which calls for the accompanying view of man as active and competence-oriented.

An extreme concern for intellectual growth especially dominates programs which have as their major goal rapidly preparing very young children from environments of deprivation to function in a school with unvarying middle-class standards. Though most programs today give some recognition to the importance of the child's having a positive self-concept, this is frequently equated with success in academic achievement alone. Yet, we know that an individual's self-concept is a result of all his relationships with others. An individual's attitude toward himself is a composite of his interpersonal relationships. While his feeling about himself as a successful school-achiever is an essential component of a positive self-concept, many other aspects enter in.

Children who live in homes touched by extreme poverty often experience a psychologically barren environment. Of these families, Barbara Biber writes, ". . . it may well be that they are really not in close touch with each other as persons: that the child has not been noticed as the particular person that he is; that adults have not played with him very much; that he has not been involved in the kinds of connections with others from the very beginning of his life that help a child know who are the familiar people, who are the strange people"(117). In such a family environment, there has been little to foster a growing, positive self-identity. Basically, these children need to learn to develop relationships with adults that rest upon the beginnings of trust and love. Only as adults give them new ways to form positive relationships and to handle their hostility and anxiety, can they be freed to learn.

Class Structure and Personal Limitations

The urban milieu has been portrayed—especially that of the urban disadvantaged—as one of persistent stress resulting from "intensely concentrated social realities"(118). For children, these realities threaten positive growth, for density of population, bureaucracy, and lack of positive affiliation with others result in feelings of loneliness, lack of empathetic understanding, depersonalization, and a hardening of relationships with others. Such devastating results demand rich affective experiences to restore identity and connectedness with others, and social participation to build confidence in self as a valuable group member.

The School and the Economically Disadvantaged. The gulf between the "teeming life of the slums" and the "aseptic content" of slum schools is pictured by William C. Rhodes as a conflict between the middle-class aspirations, controls, and renunciations required by the school and the irrational, intense, and chaotic internal life of the students. "Such a divorce from the internal dynamics of the learner," he writes, "make the culture presented to him a meaningless foreign language that can never be learned without giving up completely the content of the self, and the already-learned excitement of slum life"(119). Here, the "foreign language" referred to embraces the total cultural gap. But even the one aspect of spoken language, alone, constitutes a major discontinuity for the young child in school.

One deprivation which has consistently concerned project directors is the paucity of language skills disadvantaged children exhibit. Some programs have zeroed in upon this deficit with the specific intent of improving language skills. The Early Childhood Language Project directed by Carolyn Stern, a member of the faculty of the University of California at Los Angeles, illustrates this focus. Structured, actually programmed, lessons have been developed to help the economically deprived child adapt his language to a pattern he will meet in school. The lessons comprise a fifteen-minute segment of a young child's day in a day care center. Small groups of children are taken out of their classroom setting for these lessons given by persons trained by the research center. Language deficits are attacked as an isolated entity.

Not only this separating of language, but the goal of asking all young children to accommodate rapidly to an adult-imposed pattern, is questionable. For immature language may only indicate immature thought processes expressed in language, such as lack of discrimination abilities. Insufficient opportunities to come to know the world of things may negate the drives for questioning and probing we have come to expect in young children. Not only does the child who lacks supportive communication in the early years fail to develop language patterns acceptable to the school, he may also develop "deterrents for being able to learn in general, because it is through the active relationship with people, it is through being known and felt and understood as a person that the child's basic curiosity and interest in the world begin to flower and develop"(120). The very fluidity of speech is tied to the child's feelings about himself and others. Again, we come to the interrelationship of aspects of growth to find how inextricably intellectual growth depends upon affective development.

Another dimension of the problem of class-related environmental differences as they affect intellectual development and motivation to learn is explored in the studies of Robert Hess and

Virginia Shipman(121). Their research places learning and intellectual growth in the context of human interaction and shows the impact of significant others—here the mother—upon the child's cognitive behavior. They found a communication failure in the mother-child interaction patterns of the economically disadvantaged. This failure contributed to the mother structuring a situation so that the child failed to learn and developed a negative response to similar situations. Other negative attributes of interactional situations were revealed: a failure to provide word symbols or labels, an imperative type of control, and a restricted form of language. The investigators found maternal behavior as useful as I.Q. or social class in predicting the child's cognitive behavior(122).

The School and the Middle-Class Child. Detriments to full personal functioning are not limited to the economically disadvantaged. Studies of early socialization at the middle- and upper-class levels reveal startling effects.

Reflecting on the large number of middle-class children flowing into classes for the emotionally disturbed and the offices of psychiatrists, Rhodes conjectures that, even for them, the demands of the school may be too great(123). The middle-class child has learned from infancy to accommodate to a symbolic level of culture and yet maintain an internal personal life. Therefore, school expectations differ not so greatly from those of their home as for the child from the slums. Nevertheless, the achievement pressures to which the middle-class child is subjected may have an appalling individual and social cost. Urie Bronfenbrenner's analysis of the effects of child rearing tends to corroborate the sobering social cost of single-minded pressure for achievement. While children from achievement-oriented homes do excel in performance, they tend also to be more aggressive, tense, domineering, and cruel(124). Reconsideration of the means of socialization appears imperative at all class levels.

The aseptic content of schools works to the disadvantage of middle-class children in another way too long unrecognized. Children growing up in white, middle-class suburbia are shut off from the rich, cultural variety in our society both physically and psychologically. A four-year study "designed to learn how the public schools in a representative suburban community prepare children for a world peopled by men and women of many different nations, races, religions and economic backgrounds" found little in the formal or informal education of these children to familiarize them with the rich diversity of American life(125). Not only were the children's social contacts limited to those within close physical range, but their values tied them to a narrow view of what people should be like. Suburban standards such as cleanliness, conformity, and academic achievement formed the child's only basis for judging others and provided little ability to look at persons different from himself. This fostered a ready acceptance of stereotypes, leading to prejudice.

These are the children so readily subjected to achievement pressures and whose parents and teachers push hard to get them into the "right" college. The study of suburbia showed that the acquisition of facts for college entrance exams rules over the development of higher thought processes such as weighing conflicting evidence, making inferences, and predicting consequences(126). So strong has this pressure become, that it reaches down into the preschool. Social understanding is valued less than scientific and symbolic skills. With little to counteract them, group prejudices take root early and go deep. Observations were made of children who had learned to be hypocritical of differences at a very early age. What is happening in the classrooms of suburbia is as vitally important as in classrooms in the ghetto, for the social realities of our times tear at complacent people and institutions. No longer can one community afford to be completely isolated from others.

Parents, Teachers, and Community

It is clear that the school cannot afford to be so insulated from the home. One obvious implication of many studies is the need for more interaction between the home and the school. The professionalization of the school has all too often induced a distinct and unrealistic separateness. Such a separation was not a part of Froebel's conception of education for the young. With intuitive insight, he recognized the role of the mother in early learning and socialization. He gathered together and published a group of plays and songs to aid the mother in leading the child to a life of full harmony(127). The active need for a community of interests including parents, teachers, and lay persons was lost sight of during the period in which education was achieving a more professional status(128).

Conceptions of the interactive nature of development are reversing the trend toward separateness and pressing for a depth involvement of parents, teachers, and community in the education of the young. An open-door policy for parents exists in some early childhood projects. Still others are concerned with the self-actualization of parents as well as children. Community aides or paraprofessionals participate in early childhood centers. Parent and child centers are being established with federal funds.

The Process of Change

The change in psychological theory has been so rapid that it has produced a schism in the ranks of early childhood educators. Many, so imbued with the necessity of waiting for a genetically determined unfoldment of growth, find it hard to accept a focus upon intellectual stimulation. The split, often involving overtones of hostility, exists between those with a growing concern for cognitive development and those devoted to adjustment and the affective domain. And, indeed, they well may view with alarm those programs focused so sharply on cognition that they turn their backs on the affective domain. Such a sharp dichotomy is unfortunate for the growing individual, no matter which focus is singled out. A single-minded concentration upon cognitive growth alone promises to be no more effective than "character building" conceived as inculcation of a middle-class set of values. At all levels of society, it is the total, intact functioning of the person that counts.

National Agencies for Change

Social pressures and theoretical advances in the education of the young child have evoked responses on a nationwide scale. Head Start was the first national program designed to improve the development of children before the age when the public school takes over. It represented the largest project for young children ever sponsored by the federal government. Created by the Economic Opportunity Act of 1964, Head Start, as one of several Community Action Programs, grew rapidly. By the summer of 1965, over 550,000 children in approximately 2500 Child Development Centers throughout the country participated in this preschool program(129). After some months of operation, results indicated that a summer six-week program or even a year-long Head Start program was of too short a duration to establish long-lasting developmental gains. Follow Through became the next federally sponsored program to ensure the maintenance of gains and extend over a longer period of the child's life.

New theory and research indicating the great difficulty of rescuing a child who gets off to a wrong start before he is three years old impelled a downward extension of federal programs. Parent and child centers started as pilot efforts in 1967 in thirty communities. The program was described as revolutionary because it made possible "direct federal government action at an age level earlier than at any time before in the nation's history"(130). Its aim is to give parents the help necessary in child rearing and family development so that their child may move effectively into the mainstream of American life.

These are action programs, largely federally financed, but tailored to local needs and with large components of community involvement. They are part of the "war on poverty" via direct work with children.

At another level with a theoretical emphasis is the National Laboratory in Early Childhood Education authorized under Title IV of the Elementary and Secondary Education Act of 1965. Established in 1967, "The National Laboratory in Early Childhood Education is a coordinated research and development effort . . . to add to the basic knowledge about children and their development through research, to evaluate theories and methods which are being employed in working with young children, and to develop programs in this area based on this research"(131). As it began in 1967, the National Laboratory consisted of a National Coordination Center and an Educational Resources Information Clearinghouse (ERIC) on Early Childhood Education both at the University of Illinois and a nucleus of university-based research and development centers. The components of the National Laboratory and the directors were

National Coordination Center — J. McV. Hunt —
University of Illinois, Urbana, Illinois

ERIC Clearinghouse on Early Childhood Education —
Brian C. Carss — University of Illinois, Urbana, Illinois

Early Education Research Center — William Henry —
University of Chicago, Chicago, Illinois

Demonstration and Research Center for Early Education —
Susan Gray —
George Peabody College for Teachers, Nashville, Tennessee

Center for Research and Development in Early Childhood Education — William Meyer
Syracuse University, Syracuse, New York

Program in Early Childhood Education — Henry Ricciuti —
Cornell University, Ithaca, New York

Center for Early Childhood Education — Marie M. Hughes —
University of Arizona, Tucson, Arizona

Institute for Developmental Studies — Martin Deutsch —
New York University, New York, N. Y.

The U.S. Commissioner approved the last six centers for participation in December, 1966. In 1969, a center at the University of Kansas directed by Donald Baer replaced the center at New York University.

At all the university-based research and development centers, research in early childhood education is underway. Some are developing programs based on this research and are working directly with children.

Let us now turn to a consideration of the specific programs I visited during the academic year of 1967–68. Some are part of National Laboratory centers; many more have a wide and varying sponsorship. Since it seems likely that programs which attempt to provide for the multi-dimensional aspects of growth will have the most beneficial impact not only upon the children under their care but also upon the field of early childhood education itself, I will be more explicit about projects which plan most consistently in this direction. No attempt will be made in this report to go into the details of funding, specific locations and populations, and research techniques utilized. These details undergo very rapid change: Funding is frequently on a year-to-year basis; research techniques and even populations are modified through design and expediency. But theoretical orientations and fundamental goals tend more consistently to dominate projects from conceptualization to end results. These considerations, together with some assessment of goal attainment, are the focus of remainder of this book.

Notes

[1]Evelyn Weber, *The Kindergarten: Its Encounter with Educational Thought in America* (New York: Teachers College Press, 1969), pp. 45-64, 98-113.

[2]R. Freeman Butts and Lawrence A. Cremin, *A History of Education in American Culture* (New York: Henry Holt, 1953), p. 342.

[3]*Ibid.*

[4]Weber, *The Kindergarten*, pp. 62-63.

[5]John Dewey, "Froebel's Educational Principles," in *Elementary School Record*, ed. John Dewey, vol. I, no. 5 (Chicago: University of Chicago Press, 1900), p. 143.

[6]Barbara Greenwood, "William Nicholas Hailmann," in *Pioneers of the Kindergarten*, eds. Committee of Nineteen, International Kindergarten Union (New York: Century Co., 1924), pp. 256-257.

[7]Alice Temple, "Extending the Child's Social Understanding," *Childhood Education*, V (April, 1929), pp. 419-423.

[8]Patty Smith Hill, "Introduction," in *A Conduct Curriculum for Kindergarten and First Grade*, by Agnes Burke, *et al.* (New York: Scribners, 1923), p. xii.

[9]Suzanne K. Langer, *Philosophy in a New Key* (New York: Mentor Books, 1961), p. 23.

[10]D. Bruce Gardner, "Early Childhood Education: A Look Ahead," *Contemporary Education*, XI (January, 1969), p. 143.

[11]William K. Frankena, "Philosophical Inquiry," in *The Changing American School*, ed. John I. Goodlad, The Sixty-fifth Yearbook of the National Society for the Study of Education (Chicago: University of Chicago Press, 1966), pp. 248, 265.

[12]*Ibid.*, pp. 246, 265.

[13]*Ibid.*, p. 248.

[14]Weber, *The Kindergarten*, p. 204.

[15]ASCD Yearbook Committee, "What Can Man Become?" in *Perceiving, Behaving, Becoming*, ed. Arthur W. Combs (Washington, D.C., Association for Supervision and Curriculum Development, 1962), pp. 1-2.

[16]Daniel Prescott, *The Child in the Educative Process* (New York: McGraw-Hill, 1957), pp. 433-436.

[17]Ross L. Mooney, "Perspective on Ourselves," *Theory into Practice*, VI (October, 1967), pp. 209-210.

[18]James B. Macdonald, "The Person in the Curriculum," in *Precedents and Promise in the Curriculum Field*, ed. Helen F. Robison (New York: Teachers College Press, 1966), p. 40.

[19]See the writings of Earl Kelley, Carl Rogers, Abraham Maslow, and Arthur Combs. Many are listed in *Perceiving, Behaving, Becoming* referred to in note 15.

[20]Friedrich Froebel, *The Education of Man*, trans. William N. Hailmann (New York: D. Appleton, 1889), pp. 11, 12, 21.

[21]J. Richard Suchman, "Creative Thinking and Conceptual Growth," in *Creativity: Its Educational Implications*, eds. John Curtis Gowan, *et al.* (New York: John Wiley, 1967), pp. 89-95.

[22]E. Paul Torrance, "Explorations in Creative Thinking," *Education*, 81 (December, 1960), p. 216.

[23]Barbara Biber, "Preschool Education," in *Education and the Idea of Mankind*, ed. Robert Ulich (New York: Harcourt, Brace and World, 1964), p. 87.

[24]Weber, *The Kindergarten*, pp. 129-133.

[25]Bernard Spodek, "Early Learning for What?" *Phi Delta Kappan*, L (March, 1969), p. 395.

[26]Carolyn Stern, "Language Competencies of Young Children," *Young Children*, XXII (October, 1966), pp. 44-50.

[27]Biber, in *Education and the Idea of Mankind*, p. 87.

[28]William E. Martin, "Rediscovering the Mind of the Child: A Significant Trend in Research in Child Development," *Merrill-Palmer Quarterly*, 6 (January, 1960), pp. 67-76.

[29]Charles E. Strickland and Charles Burgess, "G. Stanley Hall: Prophet of Naturalism," in *Health, Growth and Heredity*, eds. Charles E. Strickland and Charles Burgess (New York: Teachers College Press, 1965), p. 2.

[30]Sara E. Wiltse, "A Preliminary Sketch of the History of Child Study," *Pedagogical Seminary*, IV (October, 1896), p. 112.

[31]Lawrence A. Cremin, *The Transformation of the School* (New York: Knopf, 1962), pp. 101-102.

[32]Strickland and Burgess, *Health, Growth and Heredity*, p. 7.

[33]G. Stanley Hall, *The Contents of Children's Minds* (Boston: Ginn, 1907).

[34]Arnold Gesell, "The Yale Clinic of Child Development," *Childhood Education*, VIII (May, 1932), p. 468.

[35]Arnold Gesell, *et al.*, *The First Five Years of Life* (New York: Harper, 1940), p. 7.

[36]Arnold Gesell and Frances L. Ilg, *The Child From Five to Ten* (New York: Harper, 1946), p. 6.

[37]For accounts of the measurement movement see Butts and Cremin, *A History of Education*, pp. 438-439; Adolph E. Meyer, *An Educational History of the American People* (New York: McGraw-Hill, 1957), pp. 291-297.

[38]Gesell and Ilg, *Child From Five to Ten*, pp. 63-66.

[39]*Ibid.*, p. 3.

[40]John E. Anderson, "Child Development: An Historical Perspective," *Child Development,* XXVII (June, 1956), pp. 181-196.

[41]Charlotte Garrison, Emma Sheehy, and Alice Dalgliesh, *The Horace-Mann Kindergarten* (New York: Bureau of Publications, Teachers College, Columbia University, 1937), p. 9.

[42]Clarice D. Wills and William H. Stegeman, *Living in the Kindergarten* (Chicago: Follett, 1950), p. 17.

[43]Hazel Lambert, *Teaching the Kindergarten Child* (New York: Harcourt, Brace, 1958), p. 52.

[44]Butts and Cremin, *A History of Education*, p. 506.

[45]Lawrence Frank, "The Fundamental Needs of the Child," *Mental Hygiene*, XXII (July, 1938), pp. 353-379.

[46]G. Stanley Hall, "From Fundamental to Accessory in Education," *The Kindergarten Magazine*, XI (May, 1899), pp. 559-560.

[47]Martin, *Merrill-Palmer Quarterly*, 6, p. 71.

[48]J. McV. Hunt, *Intelligence and Experience* (New York: Ronald Press, 1961), p. 7.

[49]*Ibid*., pp. 246-247.

[50]Urie Bronfenbrenner, "Developmental Theory in Transition," in *Child Psychology*, ed. Harold W. Stevenson, Sixty-second Yearbook of the National Society for the Study of Education, Part I (Chicago: University of Chicago Press, 1963), p. 538.

[51]Jean Piaget, "Foreword," in *Young Children's Thinking*, by Millie Almy (New York: Teachers College Press, 1966), p. vii.

[52]For brief outlines of Piaget's taxonomy of developmental periods see Hunt, *Intelligence and Experience,* pp. 113-116, or John H. Flavell, *The Developmental Psychology of Jean Piaget* (Princeton, New Jersey: D. Van Nostrand, 1963), pp. 85-87.

[53]Flavell, *Psychology of Jean Piaget*, p. 86.

[54]*Ibid*., p. 86.

[55]Hunt, *Intelligence and Experience*, pp. 267-268.

[56]*Ibid*., p. 363.

[57]James B. Macdonald, "A Proper Curriculum for Young Children," *Phi Delta Kappan*, L (March, 1969), p. 408.

[58]*Ibid.*

[59]Benjamin S. Bloom, *Stability and Change in Human Characteristics* (New York: Wiley, 1964).

[60]*Ibid.*, p. 79.

[61]*Ibid.*, p. 110.

[62]Alfred L. Baldwin, *Theories of Child Development* (New York: Wiley, 1967), pp. 598-599.

[63]L. S. Vygotsky, *Thought and Language* (Cambridge: Massachusetts Institute of Technology Press, 1962), pp. 104-105.

[64]Bettye M. Caldwell, "The Fourth Dimension in Early Childhood Education," in *Early Education*, eds. Robert D. Hess and Roberta M. Bear (Chicago: Aldine Publishing Co., 1968), pp. 80-81.

[65]Hunt, *Intelligence and Experience*, p. 280.

[66]*Ibid.*, p. 268.

[67]Barbara Biber, "A Learning-Teaching Paradigm Integrating Intellectual and Affective Processes," in *Behavioral Science Frontiers in Education*, eds. Eli M. Bower and William G. Hollister (New York: Wiley, 1967), p. 123.

[68]Harold W. Stevenson, "Introduction," in *Child Psychology*, ed. Harold W. Stevenson, Sixty-second Yearbook of the National Society for the Study of Education (Chicago: University of Chicago Press, 1963), p. 1.

[69]Boyd R. McCandless, *Children: Behavior and Development* (New York: Holt, Rinehart and Winston, 1967), p. viii.

[70]Agnes Burke, *et al.*, *A Conduct Curriculum for the Kindergarten and First Grade* (New York: Scribners, 1923).

[71]Weber, *The Kindergarten*, pp. 130-133.

[72]Cremin, *Transformation of the School*, p. 114.

[73]Edward L. Thorndike, *The Psychology of Learning*, II (New York: Columbia University Press, 1913), pp. 1-5.

[74]Cremin, *Transformation of the School*, p. 111.

[75]Robert Holmes Beck, *A Social History of Education* (Englewood Cliffs, New Jersey: Prentice-Hall, 1965), p. 102.

[76]John B. Watson, *Behavior* (New York: Henry Holt, 1914).

[77]Hunt, *Intelligence and Experience*, p. 48.

[78]Morris L. Bigge, "Theories of Learning," *NEA Journal*, 55 (March, 1966), pp. 18-19.

[79]Morris L. Bigge and Maurice P. Hunt, *Psychological Foundations of Education*, 2nd ed. (New York: Harper and Row, 1968), pp. 351, 350.

[80]*Ibid.*, p. 333.

[81]Donald Snygg, "A Cognitive Field Theory of Learning," in *Learning and Mental Health in the Schools*, ed. Walter B. Waetjen (Washington, D.C.: Association for Supervision and Curriculum Development, 1966), pp. 81-82.

[82]Bigge and Hunt, *Psychological Foundations*, p. 298.

[83]Snygg, in *Learning and Mental Health in the Schools*, p. 83.

[84]*Ibid.*

[85]Ernest R. Hilgard, "The Place of Gestalt Psychology and Field Theories in Contemporary Field Theory," in *Theories of Learning and Instruction*, ed. Ernest R. Hilgard, Sixty-third Yearbook of the National Society for the Study of Education (Chicago: University of Chicago Press, 1964), p. 54.

[86]Wolfgang Kohler, *Gestalt Psychology* (New York: Liveright Publishing Co., 1929).

[87]Max Wertheimer, *Productive Thinking* (New York: Harper, 1945).

[88]Edward Tolman, "Principles of Purposive Behavior," in *Psychology: Study of a Science*, ed. Sigmund Koch (New York: McGraw-Hill, 1959), pp. 92-157.

[89]Bigge and Hunt, *Psychological Foundations*, p. 291.

[90]Biber, in *Behavioral Science Frontiers*, pp. 132-133.

[91]Ira Gordon, "New Conceptions of Children's Learning and Development," in *Learning and Mental Health in the Schools*, ed. Walter B. Waetjen (Washington, D.C.: Association for Supervision and Curriculum Development, 1966), pp. 68-69.

[92]Henry Clay Lindgren, "Theories of Human Learning Revisited," in *Behavioral Science Frontiers in Education*, eds. Eli M. Bower and William B. Hollister (New York: Wiley, 1967), p. 188.

[93]Hunt, *Intelligence and Experience*, pp. 6, 106, 351.

[94]Donald M. Baer and Montrose M. Wolf, "The Reinforcement Contingency in Pre-School and Remedial Education," in *Early Education*, eds. Robert D. Hess and Roberta M. Bear (Chicago: Aldine Publishing Co., 1968), p. 119.

[95]*Ibid.*, p. 129.

[96]Alan S. Briskin and William I. Gardner, "Social Reinforcement in Reducing Inappropriate Behavior," *Young Children,* XXIV (December, 1968), pp. 84 89.

[97]J. P. Guilford, "Three Faces of Intellect," *The American Psychologist*, 14 (September, 1959), pp. 469-479.

[98]E. Paul Torrance, "Factors Affecting Creative Thinking in Children: An Interim Research Report," *Merrill-Palmer Quarterly*, 7 (July, 1961), pp. 171-180.

[99]Carl R. Rogers, "Toward a Theory of Creativity," in *Creativity and Its Cultivation*, ed. Harold H. Anderson (New York: Harpers, 1959), pp. 75-76.

[100]David P. Ausubel, "Fostering Creativity in the School," in *Accelerated Learning and Fostering Creativity*, ed. David W. Brison (Toronto, Ontario: Institute for Studies in Education, 1968), p. 11.

[101]Frank J. Estvan, "Teaching the Very Young: Procedures for Developing Inquiry Skills," *Phi Delta Kappan*, L (March, 1969), p. 392.

[102]Gordon, in *Learning and Mental Health*, pp. 49-50.

[103]Macdonald, *Phi Delta Kappan*, L, p. 408.

[104]Plato, *The Republic*, Book II, in *Plato*, trans. B. Jowett (New York: D. Van Nostrand Co., 1942), pp. 278-279.

[105]Johann H. Pestalozzi, *Letters on Early Education*, trans. (Syracuse, N.Y.: C. W. Bardeen, 1898), p. 9.

[106]Jean Jacques Rousseau, *Emile,* trans. William H. Payne (New York: D. Appleton, 1892), pp. 1, 5.

[107]Friedrich Froebel, *The Pedagogics of the Kindergarten*, trans. Josephine Jarvis (New York: D. Appleton, 1895), pp. 260-261.

[108]Friedrich Froebel, *The Education of Man*, trans. William N. Hailmann (New York: D. Appleton, 1889), p. 55.

[109]Weber, *The Kindergarten*, pp. 38-41.

[110]Nina C. Vandewalker, *The Kindergarten in American Education* (New York: Macmillan, 1908), pp. 104-105.

[111]Elizabeth Peabody, *Lectures for Kindergartners* (Boston: D. C. Heath, 1886), p. 161.

[112]Patty Smith Hill, "Introduction," in *A Conduct Curriculum*, p. xvi.

[113]*Ibid.*

[114]Weber, *The Kindergarten*, pp. 167-175.

[115]Margaret E. Eggar and Grace Owen, "Education of the Nursery School Child," in *Nursery School Education*, ed. Grace Owen (New York: Dutton, 1923), p. 75.

[116]Arthur T. Jersild, *Child Development and the Curriculum* (New York: Bureau of Publications, Teachers College, Columbia University, 1946), p. 1.

[117]Barbara Biber, "The Impact of Deprivation on Young Children," *Childhood Education*, 44 (October, 1967), p. 111.

[118]Mario D. Fantini and Gerald Weinstein, "Social Realities and the Urban School," in *Curriculum Decisions—Social Realities*, ed. Robert R. Leeper (Washington, D.C.: Association for Supervision and Curriculum Development, 1968), p. 80.

[119]William C. Rhodes, "Psychosocial Learning," in *Behavioral Science Frontiers in Education*, eds. Eli M. Bower and William G. Hollister (New York: Wiley, 1967), pp. 227-228.

[120]Biber, *Childhood Education*, 44, p. 112.

[121]Robert D. Hess and Virginia Shipman, "Cognitive Elements in Maternal Behavior," in *The Craft of Teaching and The Schooling of Teachers* (Denver: The U.S. Office of Education Tri-University Project, 1967), pp. 57-85.

[122]Robert D. Hess and Virginia Shipman, "Maternal Influences on Early Learning: The Cognitive Environments of Urban Pre-School Children," in *Early Education*, eds. Robert Hess and Roberta Bear (Chicago: Aldine, 1968), p. 103.

[123]Rhodes, in *Behavioral Science Frontiers*, p. 228.

[124]Urie Bronfenbrenner, "The Changing American Child—A Speculative Analysis," *Journal of Social Issues*, 17, no. 1 (1961), p. 17.

[125]Alice Miel, *The Shortchanged Children of Suburbia* (New York: Institute of Human Relations Press, 1967).

[126]*Ibid.*, p. 57.

[127]Friedrich Froebel, *Mutter-und Kose-Lieder* (Leipzig: A Pichler's Witwe und Sohn, 1911).

[128]Weber, *The Kindergarten*, pp. 198-199.

[129]Keith Osborn, "Project Head Start—An Assessment," in *Educational Leadership*, 23 (November, 1965), p. 98.

[130]Richard E. Orton, quoted in "Headstart Moves Down to Prenatal Period," *Washington Monitor*, September 18, 1967, p. 17.

[131]"Announcement for Proposals," National Laboratory on Early Childhood Education, March 15, 1968. Mimeo. p. 2.

Programs Including Infants and Toddlers

The belief that optimum human development is dependent upon enhancing physical and psychological environments beginning as early in life as possible has led to a growing number of programs for infants and toddlers. For many projects there is a corollary assumption: lasting benefits for children depend upon helping parents become supporting, nurturant individuals. Both premises support the Parent Education Project at Gainesville, Florida, the first one to be described.

A Parent Education Project—Gainesville, Florida

The home is the learning center utilized in the parent education approach for the provision of early stimulation for economically disadvantaged children located at Gainesville, Florida. Ira J. Gordon, principal investigator, believes that, with the American emphasis on family life, what is needed is an approach to deprived infants which maintains the family structure, yet provides experiences leading to the development of intellectual structure and adequate personality. In his report to the Ford Foundation's Fund for the Advancement of Education, Gordon states that Bloom's organization of data suggests the worthwhileness of the effort while the work of Piaget and Hunt provide the theoretical rationale. Although empirical support is still lacking, it is believed feasible that selected experiences can be used with infants and toddlers to influence and modify their development.

The central problem in using economically disadvantaged homes as learning centers is that mothering figures are frequently ill-equipped to supply the kind of stimulation which seems necessary for optimum growth. Furthermore, in the home there is a paucity of the didactic materials that may serve as auto-instructional or practice devices for children. In Dr. Gordon's words:

> The technique of using disadvantaged women to teach mothers how to stimulate their infants was developed. The task was to place a person in a home to work with and educate the mother. It is obvious that current staff levels of well-trained child psychologists and preschool teachers cannot possibly cope with such an endeavor. We created a new role, "parent educator." The basic problem was to recruit, select and place people in this new role. Since it was important that they be acceptable to these mothers and able to communicate, recruitment was from lower class high school graduates in the geographical region. It was believed that these people, with intensive training, could serve to educate mothers to carry out the kind of early stimulation now deemed useful. . . The problem may be summarized in several questions:
>
> 1. Can parent educators be recruited, selected, trained and placed in the homes?
>
> 2. Will they be accepted by mothers and be able to sustain a long term relationship?
>
> 3. Will this influence the cognitive development of the child?
>
> 4. Can the results be disseminated so that a new role is created and a new program advanced?(1)

My three-day visit to the project convinced me that the answer to the first question is positive. I had the opportunity to talk to and visit homes with these trained "parent educators," and I was impressed with their relationships with mothers, their competence, and especially with the level of professional attitudes they had attained. They were selected on the basis of four criteria: 1) experience with babies, 2) the ability to communicate verbally in an interview, 3) the ability to comprehend a short, written description of the project, and 4) expressed interest in the basic aim of the work. Out of approximately seventy-two women interviewed, fifteen were selected—

twelve negro and three white. Their general work backgrounds and living conditions resembled those of the mothers with whom they worked, except that the selected persons had all graduated from high school. They were given five weeks intensive training by an interdisciplinary team. Field work started gradually under supervision and intensive training terminated with a parent educator and supervisor visiting each assigned home. Friday was continuously set aside for inservice training. The trainees were always treated as professionals and held responsible for their own learning. They responded positively to this treatment and seemed to enjoy the responsibility given them. The high-level operation of the parent educators I met gives evidence that the training period not only provided them with specific help for the field work to follow but gave them basic understandings of themselves and others. Thirteen of the original fifteen were still with the project after almost two years. They had reached a point where they were capable of suggesting hypotheses and designing their own additional investigations.

Much of the time spent in training was used to help the parent educators become knowledgeable about and comfortable with all the exercises to be used as stimuli(2). The aim was to enable the parent educator to spend her time in the home relating to the mother and observing the situation without worrying about her own grasp of the material. The stimulation booklets showing use of materials became basic training manuals for parents. Tasks were selected which required either no material objects or only such objects as could be found in culturally disadvantaged homes, easily made, or procured.

The basic orientation of this program is an extension of Piagetian theory for the formulation of experiences which require adaptation through accommodation in an organism-environment transaction. For example, some tasks relate to Piaget's concept of object permanence. Gordon writes that the normative work of Gesell, Cattell, and Bayley were used to provide some of the stimulation tasks and to clarify the order of presentation of stimuli:

> We faced an apparent inconsistency between the theoretical position that instruction precedes development, that function modifies structure, and the reliance upon age-graded developmental norms as guides to task placement. Although the developmental norms often suggest an essentially maturational orientation, one view was that they represented, in conjunction with the Uzgiris and Hunt scale, the best data available for creation and placement of tasks and experiences. . . . The materials were so organized that each item or exercise was

> introduced to the infant before the behavior should occur according to the norms of Bayley, Gesell or Cattell. For instance, according to Cattell, the average baby can grasp a string at 7 months, so a string was introduced and the baby is encouraged to grasp it before the 7 months series(3).

Auditory, tactile, visual and kinesthetic inputs were provided in such a way that the infant received more than one channel at a time. An emphasis is upon modeling for the mother who will eventually extend the behavioral pattern to the child. Language is an important element of the modeling experience.

The major treatment procedure is instruction of the mother by the parent educator during a scheduled once-a-week home visit. The mother, through imitation of the work of the parent educator with the baby, learns the mechanics of the exercises and the general attitude of seeing them as play which both she and her baby can enjoy. The primary concern is to give the mother a sense of involvement and participation. My first visit with a parent educator was to the two-room home of seventeen-year-old Negro parents which was reached after traversing a mud-rutted road. Their first baby, nine months old at the time of my March observation, was most responsive. Both the child and the mother participated with obvious satisfaction. This father also was reported to spend time using the tasks with his infant. Another visit was to a home with a fifteen-month-old Negro child, eleven other children, and a pregnant mother. Here, the oldest girl in the family was the most active participant, though the mother watched and supported the child in carrying out the exercises. In the spirit of fun, the fifteen-month-old boy stayed with the exercises for quite a period of time. He obviously enjoyed the attention and positive support he received from the adults as well as the manipulation of materials.

In a country home a few miles out of Gainesville, an eighteen-month-old Negro girl was playing outdoors with neighboring friends when we arrived with the parent educator. On the warm March day, the child preferred staying out, so she was not as cooperative. This was disappointing to the parent educator who felt the child was making rapid progress in the exercises. But she wisely followed the youngster's lead when the little girl became engrossed in investigating all the materials in the box brought to the home visit. It became a time of extending curiosity, investigating the working of objects, and attaching labels to them. The unwed mother and the grandmother, deterred from more active participation by my presence were, nevertheless, very attentive to all that went on. In all my visits I was impressed with the responsiveness of the children and parents and the sensitivity expressed by the parent educators. The spirit of play and of supportive adult-child relationships seemed pervasive so that the exercises took on an air of gentle challenge devoid of any sense of pushing the child into new behaviors.

This responsiveness was not true of all parents, of course. The project did not hold all the mothers in their population throughout the possible time. Attrition reflects the difficult life circumstances of the deprived families involved and the mobility of their existence. In addition, the program seemed to violate some of the norms of their culture. Mothers dropped out of the project when other family members ridiculed them for talking to a baby who obviously could not talk back. In spite of the difficulties of establishing long-term relationships, enough families have remained with the project to allow the third question to be at least partially answered: The data support the hypothesis that early stimulation does pay off. Not only do the experimental children perform better upon the training tasks, but are superior on the Griffiths Scale used to provide an independent means of assessment. The investigators give a cautious yes to the question of whether or not the children benefit. The Griffiths Scales of Development showed significant differences between the experimental children and control children at age twelve months, especially on speech, eye-hand coordination, and certain personality development and social skills. The results also showed that females were more affected than males by some of the stimulation techniques.

The results have been encouraging enough for the investigators to propose a Backyard Center program for the 280 families in the present project. This would mean working the small groups of about five children as they become two years of age. Trained parent educators would play a directing role in each center. The focus would be upon three major areas of development: language, cognition, and personality. Most important, the investigators propose to integrate the affective and cognitive domains in the new program, as they have in the present program. In developing new materials, learning procedures, and measurement of outcomes, both domains would be considered. This new dimension seems to be a logical extension of the project, particularly in this geographical area where outdoor space is somewhat available and useable during large portions of the year(4).

The search for "the match" in providing effective stimuli is integral to this program. It is cognitively oriented, but supported by an accompanying pervasive concern for the total functioning of children, parents, and the parent educators. I believe it can give us sound understandings of the growth process and of the effects of training on development. Furthermore, it provides a fine model for the training and use of indigenous workers.

The use of the home as a center of learning is a natural way to improve the functioning of the young child and, at the same time, to help the mother support and enhance the growth of the child and enlarge her own competencies. Part of the study is related to changes in attitudes and abilities of the mother. Preliminary data, after nine months of project involvement, indicate that mothers improved in areas of self-esteem, sense of interpersonal adequacy, and in development of a more positive attitude toward teachers and schools(5).

The Children's Center—Syracuse, New York

Two projects in my itinerary involved infants and toddlers in their educational scheme by providing group-oriented care much in the nature of day care. One of these was The Children's Center sponsored by the Department of Pediatrics, Upstate Medical Center, State University of New York at Syracuse. The directors were Bettye M. Caldwell from the field of developmental psychology and Julius B. Richmond from pediatrics. Originally intended to include children ranging in age from six months to three years, it was later extended to cover children up to the age of five in order to maintain the gains of the program. The investigators consider the most unique feature of the project to be group care for children under three. The directors offer as their hypothesis the proposition that "an appropriate environment can be created which can offset any developmental detriment associated with maternal separation and possibly add a degree of environmental enrichment frequently not available in families of limited social, economic, and cultural resources"(6). After the first two years of operation, the investigators reported that they were minimally worried about the need to avoid detriment and unabashedly aware of the potential offered by the program for environmental enrichment.

In their effort to develop a research and demonstration day care center for the very young, the investigators wished to program an environment to foster healthy social and emotional development as well as to provide stimuli for cognitive growth during a period they considered critical for intellectual priming. Thus, they attempted to supply enrichment supplements and to forestall verbal and emotional deficits observed in deprived children.

The children in the groups were black and white, both lower and middle class. There was a deliberate inclusion of middle-class families, almost all undergoing some kind of family difficulty—marital discord, separation, alcoholism—so that day care for their children would benefit the family. The mixing of the classes was aimed at a horizontal diffusion of language style, motivation, work habits, and attitudes toward education. At the outset, only children who stayed a full day were included, but half-day children were added when this fit the half-time work pattern of the mother. The staff also included some part-time members representing thirty-two full-time equivalents and including the director, an educational supervisor, a research coordinator and staff, medical staff, social workers, caretakers, and secretaries. The health program included prophylactic and therapeutic aspects. The welfare program, offering services to parents, was considered supportive rather than intensive. While parental reactions to the project were considered to be strongly supportive, there was limited actual involvement of parents.

In the personal-social realm, efforts were made to provide consistency of adult-child contact by providing a relatively high frequency of adult contact involving a relatively small number of adults. The learning environment was considered both stimulating and responsive; indeed, teachers were "trained to use their attention as a powerful social reinforcer"(7). Trust in others and self were expected to grow in a nurturant climate and an optimum level of need gratification. A rocking chair, for example, was a standard piece of equipment in each classroom. Warmth in personal interactions permeated the classrooms.

It is obvious that this is one of the projects in which the selection and timing of intellectual experiences is a central concern. Caldwell has written that the "project represents an attempt to put to empirical test the general hypothesis that the timing of enrichment experiences may be as important as the nature of the experiences themselves"(8). Theoretically, the project refers to the work of Hunt, Bloom, Piaget, Bruner, and others as a basis for deriving general guidelines. Such guidelines relate to minimal (for safety) restrictions on early exploratory attempts, rich cultural experiences (especially visitors and field trips), modulated amounts and varieties of sensory experiences, access to play materials, and the introduction of new experiences which provide an appropriate match for the child's current level of cognitive organization. On the problem of the match, the investigators write, "Learning experiences must not remain at the same level; nor can they afford to be too far ahead of the child's current cognitive organization. They must be just enough ahead to motivate him but not so far ahead as to be out of his reach. Making the curriculum line up to this principle requires great skill on the part of the instructors." The following example is given:

> The infants learn to point to their own eyes, nose, hands, etc., and then to do the same things with a large doll or a picture. The next group, all of whom can make these identifications, learns to say these words and develops some awareness of the function of body parts. E.g., the teacher might play a game with them in which she briefly puts her hand over their eyes and says, "If we *close* our *eyes*, we cannot see." Then, upon removing her hands, "When we *open* our *eyes* we see!" At the next level the body parts will be introduced with rudimentary awareness of quantity—"Simon says touch your eyes; Simon says touch your noses. Oh, that's right, we have only one *nose* but we have *two* eyes!" Such facts will be of little interest to the child who cannot identify eyes and the nose but will intrigue the child who can identify these parts and use his hands to point, but who may have given no thought to the fact that different body parts come in differing quantities. It is probably in her skill at determining the proper "match" and maintaining it in her classroom activities that the skilled teacher most readily identifies herself(9).

My own observations revealed how difficult it is for teachers to attain this level of skill. Though the guidelines for the program relating to the selection of experience faced significant aspects, the specifics seemed an ad hoc utilization of experiences formerly tried with somewhat older children. Let me illustrate from my day's visit. In the toddlers' room at about 11:40 A.M. were ten children and five adults (one of them a male) who had earlier taken a walk outside the building. The teacher had large paper and a brush pen to write a story about their walk. There was little response to her questions about the walk, so she wrote some sentences and read them back.

> Today we went for a walk.
> We saw a puppy.
> We looked in the window of a paint store.
> We saw paint.
> We saw trees.

There was a passive acceptance by a few children, but most were randomly moving around not even looking at the written sentences.

None of the children were really involved. While they were waiting for lunch to be brought in, the adults sang "How Much Is That Doggy in the Window?" One child joined in with an "arf, arf." The five teachers were focusing upon the singing so that no one noticed a child, new to the group, who climbed up on a chair until he fell over backwards.

The three-year-old group was the one described earlier in the discussion of cognitive growth (p. 21). The children were asked to sit on a rug taped with their initials and to listen to the record of *Peter and the Wolf*. They were surrounded by observers recording the facts of lack of attention and disruption during the "listening" period. The teacher said that the group had not been responding and that they probably would go back to using reinforcement (raisins or M & M's) for participating. At the end of the recording, most children readily dispersed from their situation on the rug. One young boy, however, became so interested in the illustrations of the book the teacher had used to accompany the record that he asked for it. He found a table away from the others and spent some time looking at the pictures. The individual nature of response is demonstrated again by this experience.

The group time was followed by a second "structured" time of the morning with the children having four choices of activities: Montessori smell jars, Montessori buttoning and snapping frames, stamping letters on paper, or making a picture using melted crayons and a hot iron (a highly teacher-directed activity). A second room for the three-year-olds containing blocks, equipment for dramatic play, and other large pieces of equipment was not used during my observation. When asked, the teacher responded that it was sometimes used as a reward for doing well in more structured activities where the goal was to build persistence. Though there were five adults in the room of fifteen 3-year-olds, all children were held to these four activities. Is this the way to match cognitive structure? One might even question whether any of these activities had even a chance of building cognitive structure. It would seem that even a modicum of faith in the children themselves would recognize that self-selection on the part of the child would be much more likely to bring about a match. Were these considered growth-inducing experiences for all or any of these fifteen children? It seems that in spite of the adult-child ratio, the program seems to be searching for a spurious group "match" rather than looking at it as an individual problem.

Unlike the other groups, the four-year-olds, the oldest group at the time of my visit, were not housed in the educational building of the University Methodist Church. They had been moved to the duplex used originally to house the entire project. I never saw the four-year-olds, but they were reported to be so aggressive that they were separated into two groups. The educational supervisor told me that they were moved because of their continuous running in the center halls and kicking teachers. They were prepared to move to the new location by being told that they were going to a grownup place where "we do not kick teachers." Those who do not conform are brought back to the church center for punishment. Bettye Caldwell, herself, said she would probably turn the four-year-old group into a token economy, giving tokens for good behavior and taking them away for undesirable behavior.

Is this group reflecting the normal negativism and aggression of four-year-olds? Or has the timing of experiences been such that it has made frustrating demands upon the children which have built up open rebellion? Does the program have so many periods of restricted activity that children are robbed of a growing sense of autonomy and independence? Are the adult-child relationships hovering in a way that fosters rebellion? These and other questions certainly need pursuing.

It is reported that consultants have felt that in some ways the children's "budding attempts at the development of mastery were aborted." One consultant "found the children too friendly to strangers and possibly lacking a differentiated social reaction"(10). This was my experience, too; on entering the three-year-old's room, one child expected me immediately to do his bidding.

The major assessment of the program has been in terms of quotients on Cattell or Binet tests on which the children have shown gains. For an appraisal of social and emotional development, the investigators have relied heavily upon consultants. This is admittedly a difficult area to assess, but the project might well devote some of its efforts upon raising questions in this area and devising measuring instruments(11).

The Frank Porter Graham Child Development Center —Chapel Hill, North Carolina

Also containing a day care facility for infants and toddlers, but much broader in its scope than that at Syracuse, is the project at the University of North Carolina's Frank Porter Graham Child Development Center directed by Halbert B. Robinson. At the time of my visit, the center had programs for children up to three years of age, but a study of children through the elementary school years is projected. The goals include not only active intervention at the early years, but also longitudinal studies on a mixed population. Pointing to the fact that much of our knowledge of child growth is derived from a highly select group of children in university nursery schools—children whose home environments are oriented to middle-class values—the director recognizes the need for studies encompassing children of greatly varied backgrounds. Chapel Hill, North Carolina, the setting for this study, is a community of 35,000 people with two distinct groups: an "intellectual" element of university faculty and students and a group of service people both black and white. As a few sporadic efforts were made to integrate the schools, the citizens of this apparently well-to-do community became more aware of the depths of deprivation existing in some segments.

The Frank Porter Graham Center proposes an integration of these two groups and a facing of the social and educational problems that develop. In organization, the center is to have two basic divisions, both to represent all segments of the diverse community: 1) a day care facility for 240 infants and children of working mothers, and 2) a school for 550 primary and elementary students. The latter is to be made possible through the collaboration of the Chapel Hill Board of Education and the Frank Porter Graham Child Development Center. As the children enter the school, the Center will continue to provide a full-day program for the children of working mothers. The two major units are to provide the opportunity for continuous longitudinal study, individualized attention, enrichment programs, and experimental curricula. Two major purposes will dominate the enterprise: 1) to break the cycles of retardation, poverty, and disease by providing for optimum development during the crucial formative years, and 2) to develop an understanding of the antecedents of a wide variety of behavior patterns pertinent to educational achievement.

A "family unit" organization is to be part of the day care center, with each unit having twelve children, two of each year from infancy to the age of five. When children graduate to the elementary school, they will retain contact with their original family unit for eating, sleeping, and group and solitary play. Infants will spend their day in the family unit headquarters, but even two-year-olds will spend about four hours a day away from the unit engaged in recreational programs and special classes. Three-, four-, and five-year-olds will spend progressively more time in enlarging their experience outside the center.

This is an exceedingly large and comprehensive project requiring extensive funding and planning. Besides the Center population, there is a primary control group from the same city and a secondary control group from another community. It is envisioned that there will be numerous sub-projects with investigators from many disciplines. Care for children will also be comprehensive including medical and dental.

The directors are concerned with the problem of building achievement motivation, believing that the child's drive for competence and excellence helps him function in a school society; the child with a more passive outlook tends to fall behind his developmental potential. Arguing that children with high achievement motivation have experienced contact from early infancy with rather "pushy" parents, who have given rewards and responsiveness for mastery while maintaining high standards of behavior, this role behavior is designated for the staff. It is recommended that staff members provide for the children high expectations, aid in achieving goals, and genuine approval for mastery(12).

The program is conceived as one which will provide "novelty, varied experience, and a steady, moderate flow of input into the child's perceived world built upon a basic and supportive routine" (13). In a survey of research, Robinson concludes that "very small infants and young children are highly reactive to both enhancing and depriving conditions in their surroundings, as well as highly specific teaching programs"(14). Robinson considers the timing of experiences extremely important and states that excessive stimulation may even be harmful. However, he concludes that "it is difficult to see how pleasant experiences, stimulating within reasonable limits, can be harmful either to mental health or to cognitive development" (15).

The director has such faith in the malleability of children in their early years, that he believes a problem of cultural discontinuity may arise. He foresees a possible alienation of children from their parents because of the inculcation of different values. For this reason, he believes close work with families is imperative with the aim of developing a long-term relationship between parents and child care workers, social workers, and public health nurses. Evening and weekend sessions to explain the aims of the program are planned.

My visit to this center was brief. I talked to Halbert Robinson, but got only a quick look at the facilities just before lunchtime. The project is in its initial phase and situated in temporary quarters, yet there has been a steady influx of visitors. In my walk through the rooms for infants and toddlers there seemed to be an ample number of adults responding warmly to the children. The group of two- and three-year-olds had finished their structured morning sessions and were washing up for lunch. Their "educational program encompasses language development, computational skills, perceptual and motor skills, art, music, reading, science, and a second language" (16). These toddlers responded warmly to Dr. Robinson's entrance (one girl was his daughter) and were most willing to show me things at his suggestions. We went into the room where they were making linguistic explorations, though no one could explain what they did that morning. They showed me their Orf musical instruments and one child brought out a note or two from a violin. In a type of two- and three-year-old "unison" (different keys and different rates) they sang "Frere Jacque" in French for me. This group of five or six children were happy and responsive to Dr. Robinson.

My first-hand observation of this program is meager, but a reading of the rationale raises some questions. The program for both children and parents seems to emphasize extensive manipulative aspects at the expense of creating a sense of personal and inner growth. It is felt that something must be done "to" parents to mitigate the chance for possible parent-child alienation. However, it is as individuals gain the strength to solve their own problems and frustrations that they can become more fully functioning, and thus able to support the growth of others. For children, will the extensive symbolic emphasis in the structured session have long-range salutory effects? What happens to the autonomy of children when materials are continuously presented to them before they are ready to reach out naturally for them?

The emulation of "pushy" parents to develop achievement motivation may also be questioned. Remember Urie Bronfenbrenner's distress at the possibility of children from achievement-oriented homes becoming more aggressive, tense, and domineering (17).

The project can be recommended for the use of family groupings with children of different ages playing together. It provides a laboratory for interdisciplinary research. The effort to develop longitudinal research on a mixed population is certainly to be commended. It needs to be done. By putting the study in a day care setting and combining it with an intervention program, the problems and pitfalls are no doubt magnified.

Other Programs for Children Under Three

Reports of other projects in a recent issue of *Children* reflect the growing attention to the child under three years of age. The Harlem Research Center of the City University of New York is looking for optimum intellectual stimulation for Negro males in a study which "takes into account socio-economic status, types of training received, and the age when training was begun"(18). Training is initiated at either age two or three and is varied by three different methodologies. Sally Provence reports a longitudinal study beginning in infancy and in three varying types of living arrangements as carried out at the Child Study Center at the Yale University School of Medicine(19). The children, all from low-income families, will be either in their own family setting, with a foster family, or in "a specially devised residence for congregate care." In Washington, D.C., a program of home tutoring, initiated by the National Institute of Mental Health, included children under two years of age from two lower socio-economic neighborhoods(20). Tutors went to the homes for the purpose of stimulating the intellectual development.

The magnitude of the concern for the very early years is best illustrated by the federal support given to Parent and Child Centers. As described by Alice Keliher, it is "an effort to create some new designs to reach and serve children early in their lives, and to involve and train adults in the essentials for child development who have been unaware of the needs and potentialities of infants and very young children"(21). By the spring of 1969, only thirty-six communities were involved and at greatly varying stages of progress. A high degree of parent participation, as well as local health and social agencies and professionals, is required in planning and operating the programs. Though Dr. Keliher reports that Parent and Child Centers have a long way to go, she believes they are finding ways to reach the child and his family during the crucial early years of development.

Notes

[1]Ira J. Gordon, *A Parent Education Approach to Provision of Early Stimulation for the Culturally Disadvantaged*, A Final Report to the Fund for the Advancement of Education established by the Ford Foundation, November 30, 1967, pp. 2-3.

[2]Ira J. Gordon and J. Ronald Lally, *Intellectual Stimulation for Infants and Toddlers* (Gainesville, Florida: Institute for the Development of Human Resources, 1967).

[3]Gordon, *A Parent Education Approach,* p. 24. The reference is to I. C. Uzgiris and J. McV. Hunt, "An Instrument for Assessing Infant Psychological Development," University of Illinois, 1966. Mimeographed.

[4]The first Backyard Center began on December 1, 1968.

[5]Ira J. Gordon, "Stimulation Via Parent Education," *Children,* 16 (March-April, 1969), p. 58.

[6]Bettye M. Caldwell and Julius B. Richmond, *The Children's Center: A Microcosmic Health, Education and Welfare Unit,* Progress Report submitted to the Children's Bureau, Welfare Administration, Department of Health, Education and Welfare, March 1, 1967, p. 1.

[7]*Ibid.,* p. 20.

[8]Bettye M. Caldwell, "The Fourth Dimension in Early Childhood Education," in *Early Education,* eds. Robert D. Hess and Roberta M. Bear (Chicago: Aldine Publishing Co., 1968), pp. 80-81.

[9]Caldwell and Richmond, *The Children's Center,* p. 24.

[10]*Ibid.,* p. 30.

[11]J. Ronald Lally has become the director of this center. Since he formerly worked with Ira Gordon, it is likely that it will take on new directions including more work with parents.

[12]Halbert D. Robinson, *The Frank Porter Graham Child Development Center,* Mimeographed, n.d., p. 8.

[13]*Ibid., p. 7.*

[14]Halbert B. Robinson and Nancy M. Robinson, "The Problem of Timing in Pre-School Education," in *Early Education,* eds. Robert D. Hess and Roberta M. Bear (Chicago: Aldine Publishing Co., 1968), p. 38.

[15]*Ibid.,* p. 44.

[16]Halbert B. Robinson, "From Infancy Through School," *Children,* 16 (March-April, 1969), p. 62.

[17]Urie Bronfenbrenner, "The Changing American Child—A Speculative Analysis," *Merrill-Palmer Quarterly, 7* (January, 1961), p. 82.

[18]Francis H. Palmer, "Learning at Two," *Children,* 16 (March-April, 1969), pp. 55-57.

[19]Sally Provence, "A Three-Pronged Project," *Children,* 16 (March-April, 1969), pp. 53-55.

[20]Earl S. Schaeffer, "A Home Tutoring Program," *Children,* 16 (March-April, 1969), pp. 59-61.

[21]Alice V. Keliher, "Parent and Child Centers," *Children,* 16 (March-April, 1969), p. 63.

4 Programs for Children from the Ages Two to Five

Almost all of the programs developing in the two-to-five age range deal with economically disadvantaged children. They vary tremendously in emphasis and the factors of development they encompass; some are multi-dimensional, some narrowly single-dimensional. Some take a behaviorist approach in which the program is enacted "on" the individuals concerned; others include in their approach all the psychodynamics of growth and learning and are carried out in a spirit which is "in behalf of" or "with the participation of" the individuals concerned. These distinctions will become clear as specific programs are described.

Developmental Parent-Child Programs

Two projects, one on the east coast and one on the west coast, impressed me with the positive effect they had upon all those directly involved.

Nurseries in Cross-Cultural Education—San Francisco, California

A San Francisco community subjected to the stresses of redevelopment is the locale of a project directed by Dr. Mary B.

Lane. Children and their families from three cultural milieus (a predominantly low-income Negro community, a low-cost public housing community, and a middle-income group representing a wide range of occupations and ethnic affiliations) are enrolled in specially operated nursery schools for a three-year period. The children were enrolled essentially as two-year-olds and, with their families, will remain in the project for three successive years. This is the community action part of a five-year project carried out under a grant from the National Institute of Mental Health (1965–1970).

"The general aim of the study is to assess the effects of a cross-cultural nursery school as an instrument for promoting mental health in a community that is being subjected to the stresses of re-development," writes the director(1). A cross-cultural nursery school was chosen as an instrument for promoting mental health in a community for two reasons: 1) the significance of the early years in developing integrated personalities, and 2) the possibility of harmonizing diverse and conflicting interests when people are brought together to work for the welfare of their children. The goals of the project include behavioral changes in the families of children as well as in the children themselves. Specific goals for children include such mental health factors as the development of a sense of basic trust, autonomy, initiative, cognitive development, and social competence. For adults in the enrolled families, goals include growth in social competence, adaptability and intergroup acceptance, as well as the families' expanded use of community resources and participation in community activities(2).

"Three nursery schools each enrolling twenty families have been established. The twenty families in each school are cross-cultural—representing middle- and low-income; Negro, Oriental, and Caucasian; intact and broken families. Each family enrolled a two-year-old and plans to remain in the school for three years"(3). My own visit to the three nursery schools occurred during the second year the children and their families were enrolled. Thus, most of the children were three-year-olds and it was the second year the families were involved in the project. Of these years the director writes, "The two to five-year-old acquires his most significant learnings through the process of identification . . . Emphasis will be consciously placed upon a kind of adult response that is consistently trustful and trusting"(4). The gains derived from this emphasis were most evident in all the centers I visited. I spent the most time at West Side Courts, so I can talk about my observations there in more detail. A sense of trust in all others at the center—not an undifferentiated social dependence, but a sense of growing autonomy based upon assurance of support when needed—was consistently evidenced.

Of the program these statements rang true: "The investigators assume that personality is the mediator of learning and therefore plan to develop the kind of nursery school program that gives personality full opportunity to develop. Since play is the child's spontaneous way of learning in these years, the nursery program will be organized around play. The child in his play is learning to adapt himself to his culture with all its symbolic insights"(5). The program at West Side Courts has already been described earlier in the section on the nature of learning. It was here that some of the children investigated food coloring in water, among a variety of other self-chosen activities. There was a steady flow of effective communication among children and adults—further evidence of the growing sense of basic trust.

Each nursery school setting abounded in materials to encourage choice and autonomous functioning. The hardware of our times —cash registers, electric appliances, magnets, plumbing fittings, scales, nuts and bolts—were available for manipulation. All were part of the inductive, discovery approach to learning.

Staff was plentiful; the numbers never so great as to be overwhelming but providing ample laps and open arms for support. At one center a black male teacher worked with the children in preparing a Jack-O-Lantern. They listened to the crack of the pumpkin as it was opened up. Scooping out the seeds, feeling the slippery strands, smelling the pumpkin, and discussing the way the face should look were experiences which imbedded learnings in individual sense perceptions. Some children stayed with the experience for the entire time; others moved in for brief periods as their interest held.

Teachers exhibited sensitivities which can only be attributed to specialized training. Training was proposed to help teachers "to understand how to develop a 'match' between the child's past experiences and his present learning environment; to study the amount and kind of stimulation that may be introduced without experiencing sudden displacement and creating anxieties"(6). During my visits, anxieties were not in evidence and experiences seemed to provide a "match." A more extensive observation would be essential to determine whether teachers were "selecting materials in sequence," but throughout the visit there was ample evidence that they were "interpreting symbols of their culture, clarifying feelings, arbitrating conflicting demands, encouraging reasonable risk-taking, presenting the child's culture to him clearly, and providing 'stretching' materials"(7).

The same supportive, unconditional acceptance given to children is extended to families. This does not mean condoning all behavior, but rather accepting parents as they are and having faith in their capacity to change. That faith must be in the parent's capacity to change in response to a felt need. The role of the professional becomes that of "an acute, sensitive listener to the needs parents express"(8). Parent involvement replaces parent education as formerly conceived.

Actually, the parent program has emerged in a manner related to the concerns of families—taking cues from parents rather than setting up a program built upon preconceived notions. Thus, developments have varied at each nursery school. Some activities have included all three schools—a picnic, a film festival, the formation of a committee from the public schools and members of the parent body. Interest groups have varied from a sewing club or an art club, a noon, bag-lunch period for open discussions, to study sessions related to the care and growth of young children.

The spirit of this approach to the inclusion of parents is illustrated by this example given by Mary Lane:

> To become a facilitator for parent involvement requires us to give up many of the precious clichés and generalizations that are part of nursery school inheritance. For example, if we see a parent teaching her child to trace around a picture we don't say to a parent, "Oh, we don't trace in nursery school. That stunts creativity." If that parent comes to trust us, she'll come some fine day and say, "How come you never have the kids trace?" Then we have a good chance that she'll *hear* when we say, "See how much enjoyment the children are getting out of the easel painting? Have you noticed how fluid their movements are?"(9)

Such personal acceptance and support opens up possibilities for a relationship that will lead to enhanced personal functioning on the part of parents. Only when the relationship between professionals and parents is characterized by trust can an openness to problems and their solutions exist. In this relationship, and in the added understandings parents gain in working together to solve mutually shared urban problems, lies the hope of enhancing the living in the family and the community. At the nursery school families come together to focus upon their welfare and that of their children. In so doing, they confront and search for solutions to the urban problems perplexing them. This includes a concern for what will happen to the child as he enters public school.

Parents were participating in each nursery school during my visits. I talked most extensively with a black mother at West Side Courts. She discussed her strong support of (and involvement in) the program and her changing ability to function in community life. Such participation is an integral part of the parent program, involving indirect demonstration of desirable ways of working with children and cross-cultural interaction with other parents. Indeed, parents have shown such strength that the project is working toward the goal of having them take over and run the nursery school centers themselves—for the funding for the project will eventually come to an end. Already, at the time of my visit, they were moving toward operation of each center for one half-day per week, with only supportive professional help available. Shortly after my visit, I learned that parents had asked for a training program to help them become better teachers both at home and in the nursery school. The program was planned to meet once a week on a semester basis. If this goes well, it is anticipated that some mothers may be enrolled in a formal nursery education program the following year.

Each week every family in the NICE schools receives some piece of material useful in the child's learning—a book, a toy, a game, or equipment. This home-task part of the project is designed to help parents understand the teaching process. Instructions for use with their preschooler are included with the "task." One piece of equipment used was a balance beam; another task included many possible learnings from various lengths of string. Adults from the project go to the homes to assist parents. An overall look at the home-task operation reveals active parent participation and renewed interest in the process of education.

Data collection is very much a part of this project. Indeed, the last grant year is designated for collating and analyzing data and writing final reports. A large amount of descriptive material is being obtained. Some is focused upon the process of change in both children and adults. Family data will be derived from intake and follow-up interviews. During the time of my visit interviews were centered around the topic of problems families were having in rearing their children, and assessment was being made of the families' adaptability in relation to these problems. Adaptability was defined as composed of flexibility, empathy, and motivation with interview questions geared to elicit such information. Child data will be obtained by means of using numerous instruments including the Stanford-Binet, the Peabody Picture Vocabulary Scale, and a Social Competency Scale. Two new scales are being developed in the project—an Erickson Behavior Rating Scale and a Language Description Scale.

Teachers use a Stenorette weekly to record significant happenings that have occurred among the children or in the families. Periodic assessment of each child and his family as well as parent-teacher conferences about the child's progress are scheduled. These data will be used to write a description of what has been learned in the three years of nursery school operation.

Involvement and commitment characterized individuals in this project—children, parents, staff, director. One young male staff member, whom I had seen functioning well with children, told me about his own personal growth. Both he and his family believe he has attained a more positive sense of self since he has become a nursery school teacher.

The evidence I obtained during my study of the project supports the feeling of positive progress toward the attainment of its significant goals. Several comprehensive factors seem responsible for the positive movement: the breadth of the basic rationale, the inclusion of adults as well as children, the three-year continuous relationship, the mixing of adults and children from various ethnic and economic backgrounds. The operation of the program has generated active support from the parents. Attitudes and values of the school and home are coming closer together, thus moving toward erasing a great discontinuity so evident in the lives of many children.

Bank Street Early Childhood Center—New York City

Bank Street College of Education has a number of components, including a graduate program in the school of education, extensive research projects, and a variety of action programs for children. Research ranges from studying a Piagetian construct as it develops in children (the conservation of number), to investigating the psychological impact of school experiences (with a focus upon nine-year olds), to exploring the school as a social system. A center maintained by Bank Street in Harlem includes a Communications Laboratory making films and other audio-visual devices, as well as a Consultative Department and an Educational Resource Center to serve the Harlem school community. The latter two exist as a cooperative enterprise with the New York City Board of Education. The offices of Project Aware are also located at the Harlem Center. This is a national study of the use of auxiliary personnel in education directed by faculty members of Bank Street College of Education. Two laboratory programs for children connected with Bank Street

College of Education have existed for some time: the School for Children in Greenwich Village and the Polly Miller Day Care Center in the Bronx. The Children's School has provided a supportive, humanistic education for many years. It is further characterized today by non-grading and individualized learning. The magnitude of the many areas of study going on at Bank Street College of Education and the ability of the leadership to obtain funding for the many comprehensive undertakings is impressive.

The newly developed Early Childhood Center on West 42nd Street in New York city, as it is directed by Bank Street College of Education, will be described here in greater detail. This has been conceived as a multi-purpose parent-child center providing direct educational, health, social work, and training services to preschool children of poverty and members of their families. Begun in 1965 under a grant from the Office of Economic Opportunity, it was hoped that the 42nd Street undertaking could serve as a conceptual model for such an all-encompassing center.

The generalized goal for children and adults may be stated as furthering the positive feelings of self and others, plus strengthening academic and social skills. This may be broken down into several phases:

1. To develop several differentiated patterns of programs for one hundred 3- and 4-year-olds based on their needs and the aim to maximize their learning potential and to promote physical and emotional well-being.

2. To evolve programs with and for parents which will help them cope with the life problems adversely affecting their children's growth and educability.

3. To affect the home environment by having programs for older siblings.

4. To study and utilize the resources of the community.

5. To develop training patterns for various groups—teachers, nurses aids, volunteers, parents, and parent surrogates(10).

Here, one can see the breadth of the undertaking to break the poverty cycle by including not only the child and his family but also the social system relating to them.

Efforts were made to reach the "hard core" families—those so burdened and defeated by poverty that they would not readily bring their children to such a center. Utilizing lists of families obtained from community agencies, workers went from door to door listening for children's voices as they moved down the hallways of the tenements in the area. Not only was this a recruitment procedure, but it revealed much knowledge about family living. One worker provides a vivid description:

> We saw the disheveled living conditions of the disorganized as well as the purposeful efforts of those who were coping with and would not be defeated by the limitations of their poverty. We saw the fragmented and the destitute situations: in midwinter the lack of a coat for a child, no shoes. We saw the struggle to communicate and the relief that came with the realization that there were Spanish-speaking persons on the Center's staff coming into the home(11).

From recruitment efforts, one hundred children were enrolled in seven groups with one very small group (six to eight) because of the great therapeutic needs of these children. The school program involves a gradual orientation of the whole family to the center and a beginning for each child adjusted to his ability to stay and participate. Attendance is facilitated by hours which fit the child's needs and the family patterns, the provision of escort service, and transportation if advisable.

This excerpt from a description of first days in school will illustrate the care given to comfortable beginnings:

> School for the children began on a Tuesday for a two hour session. Class size was five to ten children. Parents were invited to remain in the classrooms, relate as they wished to the children, and participate to some degree in the program. Teachers and administrative educators clarified, interpreted, and explained to the parent any aspect of the program about which they raised questions. Many parents brought toddlers with them and these children fitted into the program with ease. Parents asked questions about various materials the children used or ways in which these materials were being used. They were delighted at being able to mingle freely with the children in the classroom and two parents said they had learned a great deal about how three year olds behave. As parents could separate from their children and leave the classroom for a period of time, the administrative educators were there to discuss with parents their various concerns as parents and residents of the community. When the children were able to be left for the major part of the school session, parents were invited to join the Family Coordinator in the Parents' Lounge to plan parent programs(12).

In developing the preschool program, the directors took the clear position that the *principles* of educating *all* young children are the same, as derived from the fields of child development and psychodynamic theories of personality development and as based on humanitarian principles. The curriculum thus encompassed a developmental approach including play and the support of children's own strivings. It is also clearly stated that the child learns best when the teacher is concerned with the affective as well as cognitive dimensions of development. The directors write, "Since we operate from a clear theoretical position about the learning process, we pay particular attention to the dynamic fusion of the intellectual and emotional components of the program"(13).

My observations in the classroom clearly reveal a fusion in theory and practice. In each classroom, the children were given opportunities and support to actively investigate and come to grips with their world through all of their senses. In one classroom a few children were stretching, pounding, kneading clay. Others who wished to join the group found the clay jar empty. I was impressed with the educational director at the center as she dropped everything to search for more clay to support the children's strivings *at once*, recognizing that this was important to them.

Though the directors of the project believe the principles of educating all young children are the same, they believe also that immediate practice requires modification as growth needs dictate. They openly search for ways to test out and modify practice long found useful at the early childhood level at the Children's School. Mistakes are made as necessary modifications are not foreseen. The director told me that in their concern for the nutrition of these children they provided them with a hot lunch early in the program. So unused were these children to sitting at a table eating hot food, that the result was food on the tables, floors, walls. So they backed up a bit and served sandwiches and raw vegetables and fruit that could be readily handled. The teacher provided the model of eating at the table. Soon, the children were able to manage hot food with forks and spoons.

I was in a classroom for three- and four-year-olds at lunchtime when a mother brought in the hot food. The children moved eagerly and smoothly into the lunch routine. The mother stopped to converse with me in broken English, asking if I were going to work at the center. When I said no, she responded, "You better come. It's nice here. Nice." So successful has been the program for three- and four-year-olds that Mrs. Elizabeth Gilkeson, Bank Street College Chairman of Children's Programs, told me she expected to add rooms for two-year-olds.

Of great interest is the tremendous progress with the families. Parents have been involved almost from the beginning in planning, developing, and operating the various activities available mornings, afternoons, evenings, and weekends. Their direct involvement is in line with the general goal to give families flexibility to effect for themselves progressively greater responsibility and movement toward autonomy. Parents have selected, planned, scheduled, and implemented a vast array of programs and activities, of which only a few will be mentioned here. At parents' requests, language, sewing, personal care, cooking, and child-care classes have been formed. They maintain a thrift shop, library, and parent lounge.

"Actually," says Hy Wolotsky, the director of the center, the parent lounge " is a neighborhood living room"(14). Here in their neighborhood, the old Hell's Kitchen of New York City, a few blocks away from their fourth- or fifth-floor walkups, parents can get acquainted (a greatly felt need), discuss common problems, support each other, bring older and young siblings—indeed, use it as their living room. At first the parents operated an adjacent snack bar, but later asked whether the school lunch program could be extended to include younger children in the lounge. It was logical to offer it to the mothers also. Now lunch is available to them for twenty-five cents a meal—for the mothers expected and, indeed, insisted upon paying for the lunch. I visited the center on Columbus Day. The lounge was full of mothers and children. Mr. Wolotsky introduced me to the mothers in the lounge. He had a personal word for each parent there—a word which gave evidence of knowing each one as a person.

Next door to the lounge is the office of the Parent Activities Counselor at the center, who plays such a large role in advising and making some parent activities possible. Trips were important to these immobile families and tended to be a total family affair. Family movies and puppet shows have been part of weekend recreation activities. Parents' concerns were expressed about older siblings, so remedial classes, tutorial help, and recreational programs have been provided for them.

The Early Childhood Center does not work alone, but in cooperation and conjunction with other community agencies. Efforts were made to open up resources and help develop a network of economic, educational, social, and health services and activities. Of one hundred families reached early in the development of the Center, twenty-four families lacked knowledge of or funds for needed hospital and clinic services, fifty-five families living in "dive" hotels or sub-standard flats were unaware of low-cost housing or overwhelmed by application requirements, twenty-one families eligible for public assistance did not know how to apply or were fearful of doing so, and nine families needed legal consultation(15). Through the efforts of social workers, these families were made aware of available assistance and were given support in seeking it.

Another example of the total community emphasis of the project is the meetings of the project director with the Principal of P.S. 51 (the nearby public school), with the Guidance Coordinator of the District, and with the Director and District Representative of the Early Childhood Division of the public schools of the city. The Bank Street College Chairman of Children's Programs is serving as a consultant on proposals for a school community program for the district under Title III. The director of the center is a representative on the total District Committee. These activities strengthen the possibilities of the usefulness of the center to the community.

Conceptually and practically, I found the Early Childhood Center one of the most exciting projects I visited during the year. Its great strengths come from the magnitude of its vision supported by carefully selected, effective personnel. It is a program which elevates each participating individual as a person, aiding his strivings for autonomy and responsibility in a way that must be instrumental in breaking the poverty cycle. For parents, one has only to view the film made in the lounge called "Talking Together" to see how they can now begin to verbalize their experiences and aspirations and to see that they have come a long, long way. One mother tells of her experiences in building up her courage to venture from the few rooms she seldom left to take her children to the center. On repeated visits by staff workers, the mother always promised to come with her children but never did. After one final visit to persuade her she tells, "I said to myself, 'You're a big girl now, you can go.' " And she did and has become very involved.

The Bank Street Early Childhood Center and Nurseries in Cross-Cultural Education seem to be embedded in positive knowledge of the psychodynamics of behavior, while at the same time open to emerging knowledge in the realm of cognitive growth. The wholeness of the individual is respected as the physical, socio-emotional aspects of growth are as naturally and as knowledgeably considered as is intellectual gain. Providing for individual differences constitutes the very heartbeat of the curriculum. Faith in each person as an active, reaching-out learner and in a perceptual psychology predominate.

The projects are comprehensive in both outlook and promised benefits. By starting with children at early ages, they are naturally developmental—not interventional. By involving families in the program fundamentally, they are reaching out on two fronts at the same time and thus have a greater chance for lasting change. In practice, they are augmenting the potential of all individuals concerned. And probably most significantly, they may be characterized by a sense of basic trust built in children, growing in adult relationships, evident in staff discussions—a trust basic to sound personal growth and essential to the educative process.

A Piaget-Derived Curriculum—Ypsilanti, Michigan

While many projects are turning to Piaget's theory of intellectual growth for guidance, one project in Ypsilanti, Michigan, under the leadership of Constance Kamii, is most consistently probing the theory for its implications for the education of the young child. Piaget's theory, derived from his "methode clinique," says very little about education, therefore its relationship to preschool education is not obvious.

The directors and researchers of Ypsilanti Early Education Program consider Piaget's theory "to offer the most insight into the development of intelligence and to give a new perspective to the educational problems of disadvantaged children"(16). The major effort of the project is to derive from Piaget's theory a framework for a preschool curriculum and to indicate teaching methods. The project can be considered an exploratory attempt to do just that.

With funding from Title III of the Elementary and Secondary Act, the program is carried out in the public schools of Ypsilanti, Michigan. In 1967–68, ten classes of ten children were conducted, with each class taught by a teacher with the assistance of an aide. The total group of one hundred 4-year-old children was selected from disadvantaged homes with approximately fifty black, fifty white, fifty boys, and fifty girls making up the distribution. In the 1968–69 school year, the enrollment consisted of eighty 4-year-olds with a similar distribution.

While the major efforts are put to work in taking a theoretical stance and plumbing it for its implications for a preschool curriculum, the objectives of the program for children are not limited to cognitive ones alone. Socio-emotional objectives include the development of achievement motivation, the joy of mastery, identification with the teacher, inner controls and curiosity, for example. Perceptual-motor coordination and the development of language are major goals in the overall framework. The work toward these goals is derived essentially from theorists other than Piaget; but the unique aspect of the project is its reliance upon Piaget's theory and the methodology derived from it.

Recognizing Piaget's basic tenet that growth of intelligence is qualitatively distinct at various stages, the researchers see the fundamental function of the preschool to be the facilitation of the transition from "sensory-motor intelligence to operational intelligence." They describe this as a time when the young child begins "to systematize his physical and social knowledge, to construct logical structures, and to reconstruct on a representational level the practical he acquired during the sensory-motor period(17). The heart of the Piaget-derived curriculum, as these investigators see it, lies in "the strengthening of the cognitive processes that underlie the achievement of the next structure"(18). It is important to point out this emphasis on underlying processes in contrast to the direct teaching of surface behavior. The study includes experiences which affect cognitive structure so that growth from one stage to another becomes inevitable. As an example, the investigators give the experience of arranging, disarranging and rearranging objects—grouping and ordering them—as a means for attaining the processes which result in the construction of number(19).

The designers of the curriculum turn to three areas of knowledge derived from Piaget which are indispensable for cognitive development: physical knowledge, logical knowledge, and representation. They differentiate each, elucidate various components, and devise teaching strategies to be used with preschool children. Physical knowledge means finding out about the properties of objects by acting upon them, observing, and systematizing the results. Actions such as crushing, dropping, folding, pushing, pulling, stretching, squeezing, illustrate a young child's manner of acting upon his environment. Since the physical world responds in a clear-cut way, it becomes the source of feedback for the child. As children repeat actions, they come to know regularities of an object's behavior and develop the ability to predict the results of their actions.

Logical knowledge is more complex, as it is based upon the internal consistency of the system itself. Logical knowledge is delineated as including logico-mathematical operations (classification, seriation, and number) and infralogical operations (spatial and temporal). The term "operation," which is uniquely Piagetian, is translated roughly as "reasoning" by Kamii and Radin, who then state the function of the preschool as "not to teach operations to four-year-olds but to teach their prerequisites, so as to make operativity possible when the children reach first grade"(20). For example, a prerequisite for seriation according to size is the ability to differentiate between sizes. Kamii and Radin describe how to begin with four-year-olds. The researchers describe games, classroom situations, and contrived tasks to promote the acquisition of logical knowledge. They point out the necessity of the child's carrying out the actions at all times, for this is a Piagetian emphasis. Logical knowledge grows only from a vast number of experiences with differing objects. In teaching logical knowledge, "since internal consistency is the only criterion of truth, it is fruitless, and even detrimental, to contradict the child"(21).

Representation is essential in the acquisition of physical and logical knowledge, for it helps the child to progressively structure his knowledge and symbolize it. It is an important but not sufficient condition for the acquisition of knowledge, for "the ability to evoke static images and words does not insure the building of such structures as hierarchical classes, numbers, spatio-temporal relationships, and physical knowledge"(22).

In representation, three forms are distinguished: indices, symbols, and signs. The index level deals with partial perceptions of an object and reconstruction of a whole from them. The symbol level encompasses the representation of objects in various ways—imitation, make-believe, construction (block building), pictures, etc. These are means children spontaneously use in their play. Piaget stresses these means of representation as the child's first step into the symbolic world. The researchers believe these levels need to be thoroughly developed before "the 'sign' (words) will evoke vivid and meaningful mental images"(23). Now most young children readily engage in imitation which is, of course, the direct externalization of a mental image. Of the children in the project classrooms it is stated, "The teaching of representation at this elementary level reveals how difficult it is for the lower-class child to enter the symbolic world"(24). The level referred to is asking the child to show what he would do with a spoon or an iron. One wonders if the formal "teaching" of representation doesn't take it so far away from the child's natural tendencies for imitation that the context is alien to him. It demonstrates the difficulty of transferring natural responses into a structured teaching situation.

The researchers point out the great value of socio-dramatic play as an activity which fosters integration of learning in the areas discussed. Their analysis of play in a doll corner shows the variety of learnings possible:

> While playing "house," the children can group dishes and clothes, order them according to size, and practice one-to-one correspondence as they set the table. Temporal sequences are taught as the children put food in a pot, cook it, put it on the plates, and feed their "children." Spatial relationships are integrated as the children arrange things in the refrigerator, fold

> the table cloth, and take the doll for a walk. Physical knowledge, too, enters the children's play. One child may take a pot off the stove and set it directly on the table, and another child may say, "Put it on a block. The pot is hot."
>
> It is through socio-dramatic play that the child fully enters the world of representation. In playing "house," for example, he uses the "index" when he has to find things in the cupboard by seeing only a part of the objects. In imitating the roles of mother, father, baby, etc., he uses himself as a symbol of these people. He engages in make believe by using round discs of cardboard that stand for dishes or sticks that stand for French fries. He uses onomatopoeia as he pretends to be a cat and says, "Meow." He constructs representations with blocks as he makes a bed to carry through his role play. When a teacher shows a picture of a kitchen scene, he gets ideas about how to elaborate his role. Finally, he has to use language to communicate the ideas and feelings which are appropriate to his role (25).

One wonders what Piaget's response would be to this direct use of his theory for teaching. But he may well know about this project, for Constance Kamii spent 1966–67 studying under Piaget, Inhelder and others in the Institute of Sciences of Education at the University of Geneva. Certainly, in the Ypsilanti project, all efforts are made to set the stage so that intellectual functions can grow through the actions of the child-explorations, manipulations, problem solving. Piaget believes this requires great patience "and time to grow, time to take in the outside world, to assimilate it, and to use it generously"(26). For the disadvantaged four-year-olds in the classrooms in Ypsilanti, is patience exercised enough? Sonquist and Kamii state that cognitive content can develop through "(a) the manipulation of the environment to induce the child to 'discover' the desired learning, (b) the manipulation of the environment to make 'discovery' inevitable, and (c) direct teaching." And they recommend all three procedures: "...preschools must use all three approaches either separately in a sequenced order or simultaneously. It appears best to begin with a period of free exploration and manipulation before direct teaching is attempted"(27).

During my hour's visit in a classroom there was nothing to indicate a pushing of children. For one period of time all nine children were involved in the experience of dripping paint from a brush onto paper. Children discussed what they were doing and told stories about the activities. One boy made a cookie jar and stairs to reach it! When they came to a point at which they wished to stop, they found their own card (sign) and matched it to a slot in a chart which depicted the activity they wished to move into (symbol). The housekeeping corner, block area, and play store were full of materials categorized and seriated: the house had seriated measuring cups, spoons, bowls; the blocks were stacked by size; the store had all foodstuffs sorted out. During a free time, children used a variety of equipment and engaged in dramatic play. One girl was so engrossed in dripping red paint on many papers that she stayed with it the whole time.

Juice time was planned around recognition of symbol and sign and one-to-one correspondence. Children were asked to find their own place by their symbol with their name on it:

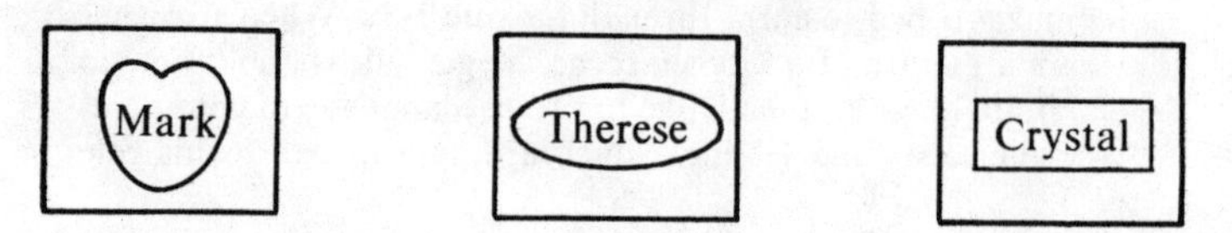

At each place was toy money. The teacher said "Today you have three coins. You can buy two cookies and one juice or save one coin and come back to get more juice." The children who came first just got one cup of juice and one cookie. However, when one girl bought two cookies, the whole idea dawned on the others and there was a rush back to purchase another cookie! Was it a realization of one-to-one correspondence or the quick response to the possibility of another cookie which brought them back? At any rate, there was certainly the opportunity to learn one-to-one correspondence.

The atmosphere of the room was happy, child-centered, patient. The one pressure in great evidence came from lack of space. In order to have the number of small groups, classrooms were cut in half. This meant that quarters were cramped; however, the teachers constantly supported children's concerns.

I can only commend the efforts to utilize the provocative ideas of Jean Piaget to determine improved ways to work with young children. This is assuredly not an ad hoc curriculum but one with a well-defined rationale, and one which needs investigation and implementation. Should it be used in such a direct manner for teaching? Or should it form part of the background understanding crucial for a teacher of young children? Millie Almy suggests that a teacher who understands Piaget's theory and has mastered his method has a powerful tool for appraising children's progress(28). With the continual concern given in the project to building intellectual structures, are the processes of assimilation, accommodation, and equilibration given enough consideration? Is there time for these processes to transpire for each child? For this project is planned to help children fit into and function adequately in a school program.

The curriculum is a constantly evolving one as the researchers continue to read Piagetian theory, gain new insights, and apply them. They see it as a difficult theory to deal with—one that will continuously make enormous demands upon the teacher—but one that will ultimately provide improved curricula for young children.

Two means have been used to ensure the successful implementation of the new program in the classroom: 1) providing a supervisory team to assist in work with children, and 2) actively involving teachers in curriculum development(29). The supervisory team consists of a theorist and a master teacher with the expectation that their strengths will be complementary. They spend time in the classrooms enchanging observations, problems, questions, and criticisms with teachers. These curriculum supervisors conduct the continuous inservice training of teachers and aides. First comes knowledge of the theory. In the first year teachers and aides were busy learning it and trying out specified activities. By the second year they were able to work more flexibly within the theoretical framework and devise new experiences.

Two aspects of the project are carried on outside of the classroom and involve parents: a parent education program and a home-visit program. The parent education program is designed to help parents eliminate those child-rearing practices which mitigate against their educational aspirations for their children and to give them knowledge about practices which will build "the skills and attitudes children require for academic success"(30). In 1967–68, the program consisted of group work with parents on a trimester format with a specific focus for each term. The six weekly sessions of each term ended with a culminating activity and a certificate for completion. Transportation and babysitting were provided to maximize parents' attendance. The content of the terms varied from behavior modification, to cognitive development, and finally to the development of inner controls in children. Three methodologies were being tried: 1) lecture, 2) active involvement, and 3) three "P.T.A. type meetings" per year. When I talked to persons working with parents in the spring of 1968, they told me they were trying to devise new ways to reach the third of the parents who had never attended any group.

By 1968–1969, those mothers unavailable or unwilling to come to group meetings were seen individually or in small groups of two or three by a parent worker. A male worker was also added to work with fathers individually or in small groups "to instruct fathers on a few of the most important principles of the parent education program"(31). The group meetings were still built around three units of study but with a methodology stressing involvement: role playing, behavior rehearsals, group exercises, and discussions. The thrust was to involve as many parents as possible in group meetings.

The home-visit program is to help parents get involved in the education of their own children. The visits are carried out by classroom teachers who teach only a half-day and make one home visit of one and one-half hours during the other half-day. It is essentially a tutorial session, with the mother given explanations of teaching goals and tasks and encouraged to observe, participate, and ask questions(32). One outcome of this program is to be a compilation of Piaget-based home-teaching activities.

This program is both developmental and compensatory. It has grown from an earlier preschool program in Ypsilanti, the Perry Preschool Project, which had as its prime goal the improvement of the child's school functioning so he would more readily fit into existent first grades. The Ypsilanti Early Education Program, to which Constance Kamii has turned her attention as curriculum director, also aims at preventing school failures among children of the poor. But Piaget describes cognitive development from birth to adolescence and gives a unique developmental perspective to the growth of intellectual power. A program which denied this long-range perspective would nullify Piaget's contribution. In the brief classroom visit I was allowed the development perspective seemed to prevail.

Other Developmental Programs

A number of programs that I visited were operating with a theoretical framework similar to the Bank Street Early Childhood Center and Nurseries in Cross-Cultural Education, though most were on a smaller scale. Among these is an integrated nursery school in Detroit directed by Dr. Norma Law and supported by Wayne State University.

Integrated Nursery School—Wayne State University

This nursery school, set in the heart of a Negro housing project, has black and white children from all socio-economic levels. I entered the classroom on the morning after the assassination of Dr. Martin Luther King. Many children were absent. Nevertheless, the atmosphere of supporting children's strivings was evident. Children were enjoying and trusting and learning from each other; they were extending their experiences and knowledge; they evidenced positive self-concepts. A few were absorbed in the releasing, masterful experience of water play. One child asked to have a favorite story read by a teacher and they found a quiet corner together. One boy spent some time sorting out toy farm animals, categorizing horses, cows, and chickens in his own self-selected way. The children went about their experiences with a sense of inner controls, while the teachers got together to decide whether the school should remain in session for the afternoon.

Parents requested meetings on a regular basis with Friday evening the time selected by them. Added to understandings attained about nursery school and about young children were understandings about themselves gained from each other. While washing dishes after the evening refreshments, parents discussed their feelings during the Detroit riots. Black mothers from different socio-economic circumstances described the fears they felt from the frighteningly close dangers. Cross-cultural understandings and mutual respect were nourished as parents met to deal with their concerns for young children.

Parent-Participation Nursery Schools and Children's Centers—Berkeley, California

Noteworthy for their integration of classes and programs are the early childhood classrooms for two- to four-year-olds directed by the Berkeley Unified School District. There is a long history of parent cooperative nursery schools in Berkeley, largely for middle-class families. Recently, compensatory programs for children from homes of poverty have developed. In 1966–67, all the programs were placed under the direction of the Department of Early Childhood Education.

Because parents of all socio-economic classes have different needs, two kinds of programs are maintained: Children's Centers for working and student mothers and Parent Nursery Schools for parents who can become involved in their children's program. In the latter, mothers and/or fathers are required to participate, attend parent meetings, and be involved in their child's nursery school class for one hundred hours each semester. In the Parent Nursery Center I observed there was a mixture of black and white children. I was told that the integration of the nursery schools in Berkeley, where the lower-class families live on the plains and the middle-class families live in the hills, was a step in the direction of integrating the total school system. This integration occurred under the leadership of Dr. Neil Sullivan in the 1968–69 school year.

Of the philosophy of their program the Department of Early Childhood Education writes, "The model early learning center must be based upon the premise that true learning takes place through a sequential process of 1) curiosity 2) exploration 3) discovery and 4) integration or synthesis of the concepts which have developed as a result of the first three steps of the total process. The responsibility of the school is to provide an environment which enables and challenges the child to work his way through the above process. The educational goal for the child is self-mastery, i.e., his ability to control and express the self and to process, in a meaningful way, the energies impinging from the surround"(33).

University Nursery Schools

The particular Berkeley Unified School District Parent Nursery School which I visited was housed in the University of California Harold E. Jones Child Study Center where I also briefly observed in the University operated Nursery School. Those familiar with the literature of early childhood will associate the University Nursery School with the writings of Dr. Catherine Landreth. The indoor-outdoor space had some unusual and challenging materials and equipment for children. A bench for sawing wood was built from an idea Dr. Landreth obtained during a visit in Hawaii. It allowed the children to kneel as they were sawing and an opening at the top of the bench gave some guidance to the saw. A tackling dummy was large enough for the children to straddle or jump over. A differently designed and greatly enlarged rocking boat provided a safe climbing and rocking apparatus. These illustrate some of the equipment stimulating physical, social, and intellectual growth. The almost international group had Caucasian, Oriental, Negro, and Indian children. On leaving the nursery school I said to the head teacher, Mrs. Sanders, "It's a lovely place for children." She was buttoning the sweater of a small boy. He looked up and responded with a dead-pan face, "Sometimes!"

Another nursery school where the physical set-up and equipment can inspire teachers of young children to provide challenging stimuli for learning is the Bing Nursery School at Stanford University. This school serves children of the University—faculty, students, and nearby residents. There are three classrooms, each with its own half-acre outdoor play area. Under the leadership of Edith Dowley, unique outdoor learning areas have been developed.

When this new nursery facility was built, dirt accumulated from excavation was not hauled away but kept to landscape the areas with hills for running up and down. In one play area a bridge from mound to mound offers all kinds of opportunities for imaginative play(34). Another has an old boat fitted into the contour. Sand pits, garden areas, and rope ladders are all placed with care into the grassy hills, groves of trees, and arbors covered with vines—making the areas esthetically satisfying as well as functional.

University of Chicago Laboratory Nursery School

While many early childhood projects are looking toward change in the curriculum, the relationship with parents, or theoretical positions, the research focus of the University of Chicago Nursery School at the time of my visit was upon study of the demands of school life and their effect upon children. Philip W. Jackson, Principal of the School and Bernice J. Wolfson, Research Associate describe the nursery school as "traditional" and with more emphasis on socialization than on intellectual mastery, if any such distinction needs to be made(35). Around one hundred pupils are enrolled in the nursery school and come largely from families which are part of the academic community. In an interview, Dr. Jackson told me that he was not concerned with "honing the cerebella" of these children; pressures for intellectual mastery are great in many of their homes. For other populations it might be different.

In their study of the variety of constraints impinging upon children, the researchers draw a vivid picture of what a child finds in school life. Even in a setting with the flexibility and child-centeredness of the Laboratory Nursery School, the child is confronted with frequent intrusions into his life space as well as with encounters with personal or environmental limitations. Teacher expectations, lack of ability, teacher overlook, clutter, crowds, and institutional restrictions are all variables within the constraining aspects of school experience. The researchers speculate on the meaning of these constraints for children: "We all know that childhood is a time of many skinned knees. If our data are correct, it is also a time of many skinned psyches. Even if most of these scratches leave no scars, they are a significant part of the 'stuff' that makes a young child's life what it is"(36). In this study, teachers will find identified many of the minor upsets as well as the major traumata to which the inhabitants of classrooms are subjected from the time of their earliest group experience.

Pre-Kindergarten Demonstration Center —Rochester, New York

The Rochester Pre-Kindergarten Demonstration Center is one of six in the state of New York. They are key centers in the state's plan to aid prekindergarten children from economically deprived homes. Each maintains demonstration classrooms and provides a variety of services available to all the other programs within its region. For the demonstration centers, as well as other programs, the New York State Department of Education provides local school districts with a major portion of the funds needed to carry out their work.

In Rochester the demonstration center directed by Elizabeth Staub is located in an old school building which has been made more cheerful through rebuilding. Experiences are offered to widen limited backgrounds and to reawaken the natural curiosity of those children who have had it dulled in restrictive home atmospheres. Children are given choice in the selection and timing of experiences. While I was there one little girl whose previous night's sleep had been disrupted slept soundly in one corner of the room. An aide was available to read her a story and gently bring her back to the group when she awoke.

Each of the four classrooms of three- and four-year-olds has a teacher, an assistant teacher, and an aide. All three are working members of the teaching team, with the aide increasingly involved in the teaching process. Besides giving assistance in the classroom, aides have been effective in reaching certain families and furnishing helpful understandings about parents and children.

Parent involvement has grown through varied activities which follow the requests of parents. Co-chairmen from the parent group itself provide the leadership. They are paid for five hours of work per week which is spent visiting homes, attending meetings, and receiving training. Open houses and work sessions are among the types of meetings conducted.

A novel feature of the Rochester Center is the video-taping of children in the classroom. One tape shows a group of children chopping and grinding ingredients to make a pickle relish. Children come and go, ask questions, look at the process, taste the vegetables, and have a chance to turn the grinder. Their interest and curiosity lead them to perceptions imbedded in concrete experience —the basis for conceptual growth. It is clear in the tape how deeply involved some children become, while others stay with the experience only briefly. In another taped sequence, the children are telephoning to one another across the room. The tape reveals the hesitant, shy language of one child, the almost disbelief of another that the sound is really coming through the telephone receiver, the tenacity of another child in holding onto his end of the receiver. A tape of children using clay puts in full view the vast differences among children in feelings, in methods of working with the medium, and in language responses.

In filming or video-taping classrooms where young children are engaged in many activities, the problem has always been to pick up the sound effectively. One room at the center was carpeted and microphones installed in various parts of the room. Though the problem has not been completely solved, great improvements have been made. Members of the staff are deeply into the task of editing and focusing video-taped sequences. The tapes do need polishing, but some raw, unedited material could be most useful for teacher education.

Early Childhood Education Study—Newton, Massachusetts

The Educational Development Center, the parent organization of the Early Childhood Education Study, has been called the General Motors of curriculum reform(37). The rambling, maze-like structure on 55 Chapel Street serves as the hub of a variety of national and international education projects ranging from physical science studies to an African education program. Among the ambitious functions of EDC are: the expansion of curriculum reform movements, the assembling of fine talent to create new materials for schools, the utilization of these materials and aids with learners of widely differing backgrounds, and the extension of work with homes, schools, and communities in fruitful ways(38). All of these goals directly apply to the Early Childhood Education Study.

Though not directly operating a program for children, ECES touches many programs for young children nationwide. The major effort in this study is to provide means for involving teachers "in shaping the places where they teach and the materials with which they teach"(39). The aim to assist teachers in gaining a strong hand over their physical environment and their instructional equipment rests upon this philosophy: "A teacher must have professional discretion and range enough to help each child become a self-sufficient traveller"(40). Workshops, films, publications, new materials, and the creation of learning environments are all geared to help teachers gain strength in shaping the educative process.

Film making of children aged three to eight in experimental classrooms is funded by the Office of Economic Opportunity. Films to help interested professionals "understand the range of complex problems involved in working with young children" are being produced. Allan Leitman, director of the study, calls them "ethological" films—films which present the ethos of a particular room, what it really looks like. He writes, "An ethological film, by our definition, is one made by a teacher following the action of the class. Over time more actions and interactions between individuals of the class are recorded. The cameraman's sensitive but subjective view brings forth a narrow band of information about the class" (41). Sequences of subjective reality are certainly made available in these films. Child feeling and behavior in perhaps a "narrow" but most significant band of information are open for study and interpretation. These films can build sophistication in observation and discussion and certainly the realization that a single series of events is open to multiple interpretations.

Fundamental to the conception of ethological films is the change factor in people—the realization that persons are always in process. The film record, as subjective and fractional as it may be, is considered "more permanent, more real, and more open to new interpretation and insights than any memory over time"(42). *They Can Do It*, a film made in the Pastorius Public School in Philadelphia, dramatically depicts the change in a teacher and twenty-six 6-year-olds over the course of a year together(43). Starting with the second day of school, viewers see these six-year-olds, who had never been in school before, grow in self-direction, joy in involvement, interactive ease and understanding, freedom of expression, and basic skills. Children's recorded conversations reveal the depth of meaning inherent in individual experiences. The teacher's brief, subjective words disclose her personal and professional growth over the year.

In the fall of 1969, a film was being made showing teachers, parents, an architect, and community workers building a playground. This learning center, different in form and play possibilities for children, will be the outcome of adults working together to create an environment both adventurous and satisfying. In its creation, it serves as a workshop for adults.

Skeptical of the use of words in telling teachers about education, those at ECES who develop publications have more faith in photographs to communicate the vitality of first-hand learning experiences. In *Moments in Learning*, a booklet using only thirty-three words of text, the impact of children learning through discovery and involvement is evident(44). *Single Sheets*, a series of pages to spark creative exploration with texture and shape, cardboard, mirrors, innertubes, mixing trays, and sounds, uses illustrations and brief explanations to free learners rather than to dictate (45).

National in scope, the study has films made in Roxbury, Massachusetts and Philadelphia; slides developed in New York City and Pasadena, California. Workshops open to adults exist from Framingham, Massachusetts to the Watts area of Los Angeles. In these workshops teaching materials are put together, often with scrounged material—metal, wood, cloth, or cardboard. A very popular film, *Making Things to Learn*, shows adults with a variety of backgrounds working in various workshops, building educational materials with a high degree of improvisation(46).

Allan Leitman proposes that a teacher must be a self-sufficient traveler in order to aid children in self-fulfillment. All the activities of the Early Childhood Education Study support and strengthen teacher's efforts to become active and forceful shapers of the learning environment. Necessary components for adults as well as children are time, support, and trust. The films show these vital elements effectively at work.

Compensatory Programs

The problem of the school dropout has increasingly been brought to public attention via catchy newspaper headlines as well as lengthy probing volumes. Critics find the school at fault in their ineffectiveness with the potential dropout and in their inability to educate the economically disadvantaged child. The roots of the dropout problem can be identified in the very early years, a conclusion supported by the work of Piaget, Hunt, and Bloom. The impetus for many current preschool programs stems from the desire to provide experiences in early childhood which will ensure greater success in later schooling. Efforts are made to develop a curriculum that will compensate for the deprivations of earlier years. For children who can no longer be reached at an early age, some plans to help them to enhanced functioning are requisite. The great danger is that in this transitional period for early childhood education such programs designed for a particular circumstance may become permanently established and utilized for all children, regardless of their background.

Those who turn to early childhood education as an antidote to the malfunctioning of individuals within the school system tend to be drawn to a model of curriculum built upon lacks or deficits. Education becomes the process of diagnosis and prescription. Even at best, this model, which appeals because it seems to promise precision, views learners through their needs, disabilities, and problems rather than viewing them as persons reaching out and growing. In a number of compensatory programs, diagnosis and prescription are further removed from the individual because the search is for group or class deficits and generalized means of compensation.

Programs intent upon the development of creatively adaptive individuals are long-range and involve behaviors which are probably the most significant for the realization of potential but are not readily observable. Some newcomers to the field of early childhood education are attempting to design compensatory programs for economically deprived young children which pay off rapidly in skill achievement. They tend to define deprivation in terms of the acquisition (or lack of it) of specific measurable skills. The goals of the project become the skills required at a given age or school-grade level, and these become the direct focus for specific training in the preschool years. Few deny that motor mastery, emotional expressiveness, and the acquisition of social skills through play are important, but the central effort of the program is usually placed upon cognitive growth. The implication has been that a move from free expressive play to more formal teaching of skills will be beneficial.

Early Childhood Enrichment Program—New York City

The diagnosis and prescription hypothesis underlies the early childhood enrichment programs directed by Martin Deutsch in New York City. He writes, "...the proper task for early childhood education of disadvantaged children is the identification of the stimulation lacks in the environment; the diagnosis of the areas of retardation in cognitive development of the children; the prescription of particular stimuli, strategies, and techniques for their presentation in order to accelerate the development of retarded functions; and the evaluation of the efficiency of the techniques used"(47). The identification of lacks in the environment has led to study of slum environments and child-rearing practices. A great variety of tests have been utilized. Attempts to make diagnosis more precise have culminated in the development of an instrument called the "Deprivation Index"(48). It is an effort "to measure the ingredients of deprivation with the aim of developing a typology of deprivation"(49).

Deutsch considers the simple provision of experiences never before encountered inadequate for curriculum building. He believes experiences must be structured and labeled so that their function is pointed up(50). The aim is to develop in the early years those areas most functional and operative in school situations, thus reducing school failure and increasing school success. Skills contributing to this goal are considered to be "the visual and auditory perception that underlies reading, language abilities, spatial and temporal orientation, general information, familiarity with books, toys and games, and the development of a sustained curiosity"(51).

The experimental classrooms for the Institute of Developmental Studies at New York University directed by Martin Deutsch are in Harlem. The Training Coordinator for the Institute for Developmental Studies escorted me to classrooms and described the program as one of skill building in the five areas of deficit they have identified in these children: language, visual perception, concepts, auditory perception, and lack of a positive self-image. The program concerns itself with the sequencing of skills, of programming material in small learning steps with easy progressions. A large part of the session for children is devoted to what they call Quiet Work Time during which children may choose from the vast array of sequenced materials designed to build skills. There are language lottos, matrix boards, name games, listening booths, cuisenaire materials, and many others. Basically, the program implies that achievement depends upon precise input.

Let me give one example of a programmed learning sequence. When I entered the classroom taught by a researcher who felt he needed to work with children in order to design materials for them, he was directing individuals in the marking of a five-day calendar. This was the first task for each child as he entered the classroom, under a flexible entrance procedure with juice and crackers made available, informally, at the beginning of the morning for these children from Harlem. Each child was presented with an individual calendar which looked something like this:

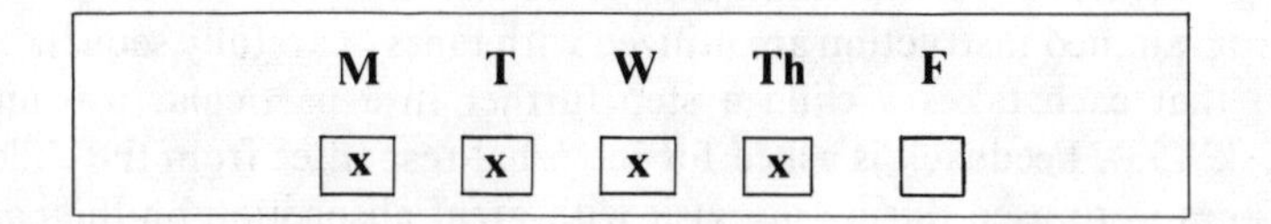

The child first crossed off the current day, Thursday, then counted those passed. There is a stamp to indicate birthdays as a special day. Later, the weekends would be added and emphasized as two no-school days, as opposed to the five school days each week.

This material is the result of a careful analysis of skills necessary for calendar work. One researcher writes, "The need to teach concepts related to the regularities of time is fairly obvious—less obvious, however, is the need for specialized approaches which insure presenting these concepts to the lower-class child in meaningful ways. The understanding of the calendar requires the integration of a variety of complex conceptual and perceptual skills, and for the lower-class child who may be deficient in these skills, teaching the calendar constitutes a special challenge"(52). The five-day calendar presented to the children was the result of analysis of the skills required in calendar reading and of devising the simplest unit to present first to children. Next steps include gradual addition of a seven-day calendar and cumulating weeks with sequencing, small additional steps, and feedback considered, as in programmed instruction.

In all of this discussion, there was no mention of the fact that a calendar is a highly symbolic representation. The basic confrontation is one of the systematic passage of time. Symbolism needs to be undergirded with meaningful experience with what is symbolized. One of the most potent kindergarten experiences with the passage of time I have observed occurred in a class planning on Monday a trip to the pumpkin farm on Friday. Some children wanted to know how long they had to wait for the trip. So they made a paper chain with four small circles and one large one. At the end of each day they tore off one small circle; they knew that when the large circle was left that meant the next day they would be off. Note the desire of these children to understand the passage of time, and their emotional investment in the process!

For centuries there has been a desire to "simplify" things for children. We talk a lot about moving from the simple to the complex. Do we really know what is simple for a child? Does it merely mean small units?

In one corner of the room were listening booths where children could put on informational or story tapes. Some have accompanying booklets about which the tape gives directions. The principles of programmed instruction are utilized with tapes "carefully sequenced so that each takes a child a step further in a particular learning task"(53). Feedback is asked for in verbal responses from the child. Tapes were used during my visit with great absorption on the part of children.

There was no housekeeping corner or block play for these four-year-olds. The room with the male teacher had a shoestore constructed with blocks, but it was not used during my visit. The reason for the shoestore was to develop matching and cataloguing skills. The teacher felt he needed to play an active part in this dramatic play.

With the extensive utilization of symbolic materials—alphabet boards, matrix boards, name games, calendars—I asked about the effect of all this on the creativity of these children. The training coordinator answered that they did not believe children could be very creative until they could make discriminations.

The importance of the teacher's modeling behavior for children was demonstrated during my lunchtime observation. I was in an observation booth which had one-way mirrors placed so that I could see into the rooms on either side of the booth. In one room the teacher, the assistant teacher, and the aide, who had brought in the food, were each sitting at a table with a small group of children who were eating enthusiastically, getting up only to get second helpings, and talking in a friendly, peaceful manner. In the other room children were moving, fussing with each other, and talking boisterously. Neither the teacher, nor the assistant teacher, nor the aide were sitting down at all. The teacher was standing in the middle of the room with a dish in his hand taking hasty bites. Though the sound into the observation booth was turned off, I could hear him say, "Sit down and eat your lunch"; all to no avail. I wished I had a camera to show the contrast.

Dr. Deutsch has long believed we can work with parents to elicit their support. He repudiates the commonly stated belief that lower-class parents "don't care about their children." He writes, "It is often stated that among Negro parents there is low motivation toward school accomplishment. I have not found this so. I've found a great deal of motivation, but lack of understanding of how instrumentally to make these aspirations operative for the child"(54). This recognition has had a significant mark, though the work with parents in the project does not seem very comprehensive. I was told it consisted of maintaining a lending library for parents and urging them to come twice a year to observe their children in the classroom.

Academically Oriented Preschool—University of Illinois

Most radical in holding the view that the curriculum of the preschool should continuously hammer at skill development is the program at the University of Illinois instigated by Carl Bereiter and Siegfried Engelmann. They have defined their approach as "selecting specific and significant educational objectives and teaching them in the most direct manner possible, as is done in the intermediate and secondary school grades"(55). Language, reading, and arithmetic are the "subject" areas in which they believe a child must gain rapid proficiency in order to succeed in elementary school.

Picture an average-sized classroom containing essentially tables, chairs, and a piano from which the space for three smaller rooms has been subtracted. It is in these three small, completely partitioned cubicles that children spend an hour a day in groups of four to five with a teacher. The three spaces are for the three types of "lessons"—arithmetic, language, and reading. One teacher presents the language lessons to all the children, another arithmetic to all, and the third one reading to all. The children move from cubicle to cubicle "as they would in a departmentalized high school"(56).

The dialogue is simple to follow, for it moves from teacher to child in a steady pattern as the teacher searches for a single, right answer. This is illustrated by a brief verbatim excerpt from a language lesson I observed. Five children are responding to a young female teacher:

> Teacher: What am I talking about? Sunday, Monday, Tuesday, Wednesday, Thursday, Friday.
> Children in unison: Days of the week.
> Teacher: You are so good. Let me shake your hands. What am I talking about? January, February, March, April, May, June.
> Children: Months of the year.
> Teacher: You are so smart. What is the opposite of smart?
> Children: Dumb.
> Teacher: Dumb is the opposite of smart. What is the same as beautiful?
> Children: Pretty.
> Teacher: Good. You are so good. If someone is beautiful they are pretty. What is the opposite of pretty?
> Children: Ugly.
> Teacher: I'll have to shake everyone's hand. He's not strong, he's weak. What's the opposite of weak?
> Children: Strong.
> (And so on through starved is the same as hungry, skinny is the same as thin, hard is the same as difficult.)

All of this was done in an intensive, fast-paced manner with the young teacher literally shouting at the children and the children shouting their responses.

Part of my observation of this program was described earlier in the section on the nature of learning. "Lesson" after "lesson" evidenced the learning process as operant conditioning. Learning was divided into a number of small tasks and reinforced one by one. Operants—sets of acts—were continually reinforced by crackers on the day I observed. As one group of five-year-old children was being drilled on arithmetic facts and finding answers by recourse to a chart, a trainee of the program observing the lesson asked after each response, "Are you smart?" As the child responded, "Yes, I am smart," she popped a cracker in his mouth.

Not only is positive reinforcement utilized, but negative reinforcement forces children to drop behavior not acceptable in the classroom. Punishment is considered necessary in order to clarify the rules of the school situation. The originators of the program wrote, "The purpose of punishment is to deter the child from behaving in an undesirable way. The punishment should therefore be designed to 'outweigh' the gratification the child derives from misbehaving. Punishment, in other words, should hurt"(57). A slap or a good shake by the teacher is recommended for "unrestrained, unthinking physical behavior" on the part of the child. For "calculated" misbehavior (i.e., clowning during a study period) isolation is prescribed. It is recommended that the isolation room be unpleasant to be effective. There is a small, poorly lighted closet with only a chair in the basement of the Colonel Wolfe school where this drill program is housed.

For many years teachers tried to overwhelm children into learning—with birch rods and other negative reinforcers. Fear has not proven to be the stimulus for lasting learning, but the best way to negate an active desire to learn. If these children came with curiosity, initiative, or a questioning attitude, such behavior would be squelched by these procedures which demand instead a child who is passive except in response to the teacher, conforming to adult standards and rules and adept at discerning and following adult directions. As pointed out earlier, the learning in this classroom is based on a view of the learner as non-purposive. It also assumes that intellectual growth can be divorced from affect.

The program bases its claims to success upon contentions of raising the I.Q's of children. Bereiter and Engelmann argue that their direct instruction program is essentially the only one that does this effectively(58). Most other arguments they dismiss as not relevant to preparing children for elementary school, the only goal they consider.

One might even question whether the children are learning the facts as the program supposes. Of course, they can repeat in verbalized form those facts that have been drilled into them. Early childhood specialists know how easy it is for children to develop pseudo-concepts—verbalizations with no concrete meaning and no transferability to new situations. We do know that absence of many and varied concrete experiences to provide meaning for symbolic manipulations may hinder the adequate development of abstract thinking and possibly place limits on reading comprehension. The rote emphasis of the program is absolutely opposed to Piagetian theory with its emphasis upon assimilation and equilibration. The directors of the program place no claim upon emerging theoretical positions. Rather, they seem to be moving counter to new theoretical developments.

Interestingly, Constance Kamii and Louise Derman personally tested some children taught by Siegfried Engelmann—not disadvantaged children but those in the University of Illinois laboratory school. Following his conviction that skills can be directly taught, including the Piagetian constructs of conservation, specific gravity, and judgment of speed, Englemann taught these children rules related to these phenomena. Children were then to apply rules learned verbally to observable phenomena. While the children used the rules well in some test situations, further probing revealed inconsistencies and limited understanding of the phenomena. The sensorimotor roots of logical and physical knowledge was evidenced further by the children's attempts to use the overlay of rules in ways unsupported by the data and their final resort to sensorimotor and intuitive modes of operating(59). While the rules these children were taught seemed an expediency which gave immediate answers, well-grounded meaning was lacking for them. Only through long-term development of cognitive processes do logical and physical knowledge become integrated into the thought structure of the child for flexible, adaptable use.

Pertinent here are William Martin's comments about the effects of sensory deprivation on cognitive functioning. Without sensory experiences—external stimulation—the child has no way of "checking, monitoring or verifying his cognitive model of the environment"(60). To deprive the child of rich and constantly changing interaction with the world of things reduces him to the helpless state of depending upon the verbalizations of others.

Incidentally, there were four other programs for young children in operation at the University of Illinois. Two others at the Colonel Wolfe school, where the Bereiter-Engelmann program was housed, were also behavioristic, intervention programs. One directed by Dr. S. W. Bijou was essentially programmed instruction in skill learning, highly dependent upon reinforcement, both negative and positive. The other directed by Merle B. Karnes contained structured periods in "subject" areas. A third program was the developmentally oriented nursery school in the Child Development Institute.

Finally, a classroom for disadvantaged four-year-olds was housed in a public school and directed by Dr. Bernard Spodek as part of an Experienced Teacher Fellowship Program. These programs represent in microcosm the divergent programs existing in our country.

Liverpool Laboratory School—Syracuse, New York

My introduction to the program at the Liverpool Laboratory School occurred in a staff meeting which I was invited to join. This Laboratory School was maintained and directed by the Research and Development Center in Early Childhood Education at Syracuse University in New York. William J. Meyer was the Center Director. The school had six classrooms of four-year-olds, all from the Liverpool community which is adjacent to Syracuse. These children were not economically deprived, but were essentially from suburban homes. Dr. Meyer makes the valid point that not all ongoing research should be using deprived populations—that there is a tremendous amount we need to know about the growth and learning of all children. Why then is this program categorized under compensatory programs? Because the prime concern seemed to be cognitive intervention. Investigators seemed intent upon deriving a new timetable for children's performance of certain tasks; indeed, to see whether or not they could get them to perform tasks earlier and earlier. It was here that the shoe-tying episode, recounted previously, occurred.

The staff meeting revealed extensive dissension. Teachers were resisting demands of administrators and program designers. They disliked being involved in pushing children to achieve tasks at younger ages. Teachers were especially opposed to the reinforcement procedures forced upon them. The following is an excerpt from the precise sequence they were resisting:

> The Reinforcement Sequence
>
> The reinforcement sequence is designed to be appropriate to any of the learning series. Its value lies in the fact that it should facilitate learning because the use of contingent reinforcement gives the learner immediate positive feedback concerning the correctness of his performance. In addition since the teacher is the reinforcement dispenser, she becomes the children's center of attraction which again should facilitate the learning process in that the learners will be more attentive to her directives.

> For reinforcement to be an effective incentive, it must be administered immediately and consistently. These requirements place strong demands on the teacher in the sense that she must be constantly aware of the overt behavior of the children she is dealing with. Although these demands are great, the rewards are just that much greater.
>
> There will be four steps to the sequence..........
>
> Step I.
>
> Each correct response unit will immediately be rewarded with one M and M candy or raisin.
>
> Step II.
>
> Each correct response unit will receive one token (poker chip) or predetermined number of them that may be traded at the end of the session for a small prize (ring).
>
> Step III.
>
> Each correct response unit will receive one token which at the end of the session will be traded for a more valuable token. As soon as C has two or more valuable tokens, he may trade them for a prize.
>
> Step IV.
>
> Same as step III except that C will now need four tokens to receive a prize(61).

The outline for the reinforcement sequence was given to me by a doctoral student in psychology responsible for the designing of the curriculum. Units designed by him for use by teachers included: Color Learning, Visual-Motor Template Forms, Number, Telling Time. Steps in presentation were minutely worked out—programmed. Notes to the teacher in the Telling Time Unit included: "Each child will have a mini-clock while T will use a large demonstration clock. . . . In general, directions concerning 'doing' should be done by the entire group at one time. Those involving 'saying' should be done with each child in turn . . . . In those sections calling for the teacher to move the hand of the clock with the child's finger on it, it may be just as well for the child simply to imitate on his clock what T has modeled on hers"(62).

Obviously, the program includes a behaviorist approach with operant conditioning the learning process utilized. It is apparent that the program designers are searching for stimuli to get children to perform at their demand. The demands seem to relate less to cognitive processes than to specific knowledge or skills. The skills of visual discrimination, language, perceptual-motor ability and attention are made the objectives of specific programs and utilized with children in thirty-minute lessons, one per day. Children's inability to concentrate during the lesson periods led to the use of external reinforcements with the M & M's and raisins extended to tokens for these four-year-olds. Externality characterizes both the content and the process of these lessons.

Are these investigators seeking a spurious four-year-old "match"? They hardly seemed to be aware of the uniqueness of individual children and their particular growth trends. In the shoe-tying incident there were three adults in the classroom of fifteen children, yet all children *had* to begin their morning with the task—easy for some, satisfying for at least one, but frustrating for others. The same child who had found the shoe-tying impossibly frustrating was asked to end his morning in a group with the Telling Time Unit. He refused to do anything with his mini-clock. When I pointed out to the curriculum designer the nature of the child's day, his response was "Oh, he can do this. He just won't."

Why wouldn't the young boy become an active participant in the group? What developments in the affective realm were constituting blocks to his involvement? Can operant conditioning be coupled with some concern for the affective side of growth? It doesn't seem that it can. By its very nature—doing something to what is considered a passive organism—it turns its back upon these significant realms. Indeed, the addition of extrinsic reinforcement seems to entail a psychological coercion which few children can withstand regardless of their inner feelings.

The investigators believe that the children under their care will possess cognitive capabilities "beyond that of the typical kindergarten child." Thus, they believe they must work with kindergarten teachers to modify the program to adjust to the children. Is an operant-conditioning program envisioned for the next step also? The investigators write, "Our experience shows, so far, that these children are thriving in the stimulating environment provided and that planning is needed to maintain the children's current developmental progress"(63). Yet they present no evidence of how these children are "thriving" or indeed, what "thriving" means to them. With a philosophical dichotomy existing between those who designed the program and those who carried it out, any suggested results need careful scrutiny.

The New Nursery School—Greeley, Colorado

Like many of the projects discussed, the New Nursery School is a complex operation. It is very difficult, perhaps impossible, to give the essence of it briefly. The directors say the program is based upon a combination of the ideas of Maria Montessori, Omar Khayyam Moore, and Martin Deutsch. In this respect, of course, it is not new, though the combination of ideas may be somewhat unique. Dr. Glen Nimnicht, the original director, came into nursery education to try to prevent Spanish-American children from beginning the failure process in kindergarten and first grade. He was formerly a principal in a junior high school in a small Wyoming town(64). The nursery school that developed serves mainly three- and four-year-old children with Spanish surnames.

The first thing the staff at the New Nursery would have you know about the school is that it is organized as an autotelic responsive environment. Autotelic refers to activity done for its own sake rather than for obtaining rewards or punishments that have no inherent connection with the activity itself. Choice by the learner is honored, thus eliminating the "fear of pushing the child beyond his capacity"(65). A child can spend as much time with one activity as he likes, with no one asking him to stop the activity to begin another. A statement follows from this exploration of autotelic choice, the point of which is clear to many early childhood educators:

> These children do have a short attention span if they are required to do what the adult wants to do when the adult wants to do it. But when the children are allowed to choose their own activities this no longer holds. Many children have been read to for an hour and a half. One child painted 25 pictures without stopping. Another spent the whole three hours except for time out for refreshments, playing a game which required him to recognize and match pictures(66).

Such wonderful persistence! It dispels the myth of short attention span.

A responsive environment must be prepared so that the learner is immediately informed about the consequences of his actions. This desire for responsiveness gives directives for the kinds of equipment that is provided and for the behavior of the teacher and her assistants. Toys and equipment are selected which allow the child to work with them individually and freely and are self-corrective. Nesting and stacking toys go together in only one way; puzzles do the same. The Bell and Howell Language Master talks back to the child.

For the adults in the environment, their responsive role requires the following specific behaviors:

1. Discourage adult initiated conversation but encourage child initiated conversation;
2. Never ask a child if he wants to be read to but always read to him when he asks to be read to;
3. Avoid asking a child to give up one activity to do something else;
4. Never insist that any children come to a group activity(67).

In general, these autotelic responsive factors were in evidence during the afternoon session when I watched from the observation booth. There were fifteen children—threes and fours mixed—with a head teacher and two Head-Start trainees in an eight-week training program. Several boys spent almost all of the afternoon up to group time in the block area. There was an abundance of helmets and hats which they utilized for their dramatic play. There was great interchange of language from child to child, which I was unable to pick up in the observation booth. Other children were at a table using blue and yellow colors set out for sponge painting. Others at the same table were dropping blue and yellow coloring into water with an eyedropper. A teacher was reading a story to three children. Two children were occupied with the Language Master. One was sorting pine cones by size. Later, puzzles and other color and shape sorting materials were utilized.

During this time, except for one instance, I saw no adult-initiated conversations. Indeed, it seemed to me that the adults essentially acted as mediators of the environment with minimal child contact. Therein lies one of the greatest doubts I have about this program with many fine features. It seemed to lack the warmth and supportive personal relationships so essential for building trust and responsiveness returned. There certainly was regard for children, but little positive expression of it. Incidentally, one of the directors of the program complained to the teacher that the Head Start trainees seemed cold and withdrawn from the children. I observed nothing which provided a model for them of warmth and loving regard, even with these tremendously appealing children.

The free-choice period was followed by a story time which all the children willingly joined. For the first time the young teacher sparkled with enthusiasm as she told a story about a child who went to school dressed in green trousers, blue shirt, and red hat after eating an orange and a brown egg. The clothes and food were illustrated in colored paper which the children later matched with colored squares. Directions to go outside were given in terms of the colors in the clothing children were wearing. It was a didactic fifteen-minute group time, which seems to be very much part of the total program. Film clips being made at the nursery school as training units illustrate very didactic group times where the learning of concepts of color and size, or same and not same, or sound perception form the objectives. How do these become a part of a program based upon autotelic and responsive notions? Or do the directors feel such didactic "lessons" are necessary, imbedded in the larger periods of choice? Much attention seems to be given to inculcating such concrete and measurable concepts as color, shape, numbers, patterns, etc. Concept-formation ability is one of the four intellectual aspects of growth identified in the program, along with development of the senses and perceptual acuity, language ability, and problem-solving ability(68).

A procedure recommended for language development seemed at odds with the autotelic responsive environmental orientation. During their time in the small, poorly equipped outdoor area, the children were subjected to a kindly, but constant verbal bombardment. The nearby teacher put into words the motor activities of the children. I failed to take down a verbatim account, but it was close to this sequence suggested for use over a period of time:

> Juanita slides down the board!
> Juanita is sliding down the board!
>
> ---
>
> Juanita slides down the board backwards!
>
> ---
>
> Juanita, do you want to slide down the board or run down the board?(69)

During outdoor play the teachers continuously verbalized a child's activity—not, certainly, at the request of the child. The same procedure had prevailed indoors at the table where children had been sponge-painting and dropping colors into water.

Throughout the afternoon session individual children were invited by an adult to go to booths equipped similarly to those devised by O. K. Moore. A description of the booth experience will be included later, but I would like to comment on the major objectives of using the booths where an electric typewriter is the central piece of equipment. These objectives are stated as the development of language skills and problem solving. For example, if, in the booth, a child is shown a letter *b* and finds it on the typewriter, it is considered that he has solved a problem. Or, in the classroom, if a child is shown papers of various colors and sizes and he can give, at the teacher's request, the large green triangle, this is called problem solving. Both are certainly indicative of perceptual attainment and ability to follow directions. Can they be properly termed problem solving? For specific reasons, I believe not. Problem solving in a broader sense requires that the learner recognize a problem to be solved, thus setting his own goals and thereby being able to know when it is solved, for his goal is reached. For example, a child setting out to build a toy airplane at the workbench knows how he believes it should look. When he has put it together to suit his conceptual model, he has solved his problem—no matter what others might think of it. Or, in another instance, a young child running along pulling a wagon behind him in order to help his friend gather stones catches one wheel on a boulder impeding his progress. When he learns how to disengage the wheel, perhaps by backing the wagon up, or by lifting it over, he has solved a recognized problem and knows it is solved when he can go on. This is problem solving in the Deweyan sense, with the learner setting out to accomplish a task with his own goals before him, taking steps to reach the goals, and knowing when they have been achieved. The evaluation is imbedded in the goal setting.

Two-thirds of the 1967 Progress Report on the New Nursery School is devoted to discussion of testing procedures. The Stanford-Binet, the Peabody Picture Vocabulary Test, a Preschool Inventory developed at the Children's Center in Syracuse, and a Cincinnati Autonomy Test are described. The researchers were looking for trends which indicated through pre- and post-testing that the nursery school children were growing in intellectual capacity. Increases in mean I.Q. scores and on the PPVT were evident. The other results are more complex. Three tests developed in the project are described: a category test, one based upon classification systems, and a simple test of ability to name basic colors.

In this project there has been no extensive work with parents, although the investigators are aware of some of the values of including them. During one of the two meetings set up per year, parents were shown a film of their children in the nursery school. Some parents objected to their children being shown on films made for wide distribution!

CUE Study—New York City

Based upon a different curriculum rationale is the study of intellectual stimulation of disadvantaged prekindergarten children sponsored by the Center for Urban Education in New York City. Of the rationale for the study, the original researchers, Kenneth D. Wann and Helen F. Robison, wrote:

> In this study, intellectual stimulation is conceived as a collection of input variables which require the child to engage in a range of cognitive activities. The most basic sources of intellectual stimulation are assumed to be the disciplines of knowledge, as defined, organized and structured by scholars in each discipline. Hence, the content selected as intellectually stimulating for the young child is drawn from selected disciplines here regarded as most appropriate and accessible for the young child's initial encounters with some of man's most fundamental conceptualizations and ways of knowing(70).

The researchers point out that they do not intend to eliminate traditional goals of physical, social, and emotional growth, but rather to add and facilitate intellectual development as accentuating the school's major commitment.

In 1966–67, the population of the study consisted of nine prekindergarten classes (for four-year-olds) in four special service schools in New York City. These classes included about one hundred and thirty children, nine teachers, plus the teacher aides and family workers assigned to the classes. When I visited in 1967–68, Dr. Wann had left Teachers College so Helen Robison was continuing the work in four prekindergarten classrooms in two schools. Much of the effort has gone into developing detailed materials for teachers, mapping (as it were) as many elements as possible which are considered to help them maintain an intellectually stimulating classroom climate. Games and materials have been devised. For example, a nodal game has been created to elicit geographic concepts: strips of white paper to be laid out on the floor of the classroom so that they criss-cross each other to form streets. Children and teacher are to walk on the streets. When they get into all kinds of congested patterns, they work out a solution. Perhaps a trip to the street corner to see how traffic is regulated may follow.

As in other programs, these researchers consider that a systematic curriculum requires a variety of learning experiences. The terms "play-centered learning," "planned experiences," and "sequentially structured episodes" are given to the three types. During my visit to a classroom in Harlem I observed a great deal of play-centered learning by individuals and small groups. About twenty children with a teacher, aide, and parent were working together in a seemingly comfortable relationship. In the block corner complex structures were growing; dramatic play was absorbing some children in the housekeeping corner; play-dough, paper, and crayons were being used by others. One boy, formerly very shy, came to a teacher continually to explain what he was pretending to cook in toy dishes. Four children with earphones were sitting at a table and listening to a tape made previously when they were in the housekeeping corner. These four children were having an animated discussion of the tape: "You were there." "We were using the dishes." One little girl having some difficulty with temporal relationships asked, "Is I there now?" This response in listening to the tape is a great advance for these children. In the beginning of the year when a teacher inadvertently put on an empty tape, children sat passively for some time. Finally one child said to a teacher, "I don't hear nothin'."

A planned, more structured experience occurred before juice time while many children were still cleaning up the room. The teacher instructed a few children to play a Vinyl Tile game requiring children to stop and place a plastic disc on certain colored tiles according to a specific direction. This game had a rather complex set of directions which the children had not grasped. The game was to help children gain a sense of one-to-one relationship and patterning, but on this day the patterning seemed difficult for many.

Mid-morning lunch time was very structured with the teacher asking, "I have a cup. Do you have a cup? How many cups do you have?" This came close to verbal bombardment, as children were expected to respond quickly.

An observer must ask himself many questions: When the teacher takes over all the conversation at juice time, doesn't this eliminate vital spontaneous conversation by the children? Does it add to their passivity? When many planned, structured experiences are added to a program and seem to hold rather high priority, what happens to learning through play? Some project teachers were asking how they could take advantage of experiences that spontaneously arise in the classroom or outside when they felt held to following a definitely sequenced program. Vital questions about sequencing versus continuity in learning are raised here. All the dilemmas arising from structuring learning precisely for very young children come to focus in this program. Some very interesting games and materials may develop from the investigation of using key concepts from various disciplines to open up experiences for children. Does more freedom need to be allowed in their use? Or do teachers need to develop more judgment in selecting and presenting experiences?

Teachers and researchers have regular meetings to discuss experimental materials and their use with children. Video-tapes were made of structured lesson sequences. These have been successful as a means of aiding teachers; they recognize many aspects of their own behavior they wish to change.

Preschool Curriculum Demonstration Project—Ypsilanti, Michigan

Ypsilanti is a community of about 25,000 on the fringe of the metropolitan Detroit area. David Weikart, the prime mover of projects for young children in this area, gives a description of the town. "The community has the lowest tax base of any unit in the county. As housing is cheaper in Ypsilanti than surrounding communities and as the city has the only public housing in the county, many working class families have settled in the city though they may work elsewhere. About 25 percent of the Ypsilanti population is Negro with few in the middle class or above"(71).

The children in the first project, the Perry Preschool Project, Weikart designated as "Negro, culturally deprived and diagnosed as mentally retarded"(72). The latter designation rested upon the interpretation of scores obtained from Stanford Binet tests (and its downward extension, the Cattell Infant Intelligence Scale) administered to three- and four-year-olds. Even though the scores were regarded as a function of cultural deprivation, it was considered that the children tested in the range of "educably mentally retarded"(73).

With such labeling one would expect to find an instructional program compensatory in nature and designed to remedy what were considered cognitive deficits. Early programs included extensive verbal bombardment. Later programs were described as an implementation of Piaget's cognitive development theory. There is much statistical data available relating to the Perry Preschool Project as it was developed and operated by David Weikart, Constance Kamii, and Norma Radin. By the time of my visit, Constance Kamii and Norma Radin were engaged in implementing the Piaget-Derived Curriculum Project and David Weikart was directing a Preschool Curriculum Demonstration Project. In the latter, three differing preschool curricula were studied and compared.

The Ypsilanti Preschool Curriculum Demonstration Project is designed essentially to demonstrate which of three "curricula styles" best raises the level of functioning of the three- and four-year-old children designated as disadvantaged and functionally retarded. David Weikart writes:

> The preschool field has now reached a point at which the relatively successful curricula must be pulled together in a demonstration project to determine the assets of each. It is only through such an attempt that the comparative advantages of each can be identified and documented. This effort would provide a wealth of material and information which would be of highest importance to the entire preschool field(74).

The researchers talk continuously about "curricula styles." By this, they really refer to differing goals, rationales, and classroom procedures. They never consider differing teacher styles within a given program, though this may be one of the major weaknesses of the entire endeavor.

The whole project is placed in a research framework. It is another project which considers that something must be done to these children—and their parents—to compensate for labeled deficits and "functional mental retardation." Thus, emphasis in the proposal is upon obtaining research data or evidence.

> The success of the four (later limited to three) preschool curricula will be evaluated through the use of pre-, post-, and follow-up testing of the child. The groups will be matched for general intellectual functioning and placed into equal groups at the start of the program. Differences in the outcome of the programs will be evaluated through the use of standardized individual intelligence tests, teacher ratings, supervisor ratings, and achievement tests administered at the end of the preschool and kindergarten year(75).

The three classrooms have some common factors. They have small groups of sixteen 3- and 4-year-olds with at least two teachers for a half-day session five days a week. Each program has a home teaching component. A participating family will be visited once every other week by the classroom teacher. In this session the mother is to be trained in methods to aid directly in the intellectual development of her child. The home content material is based upon the particular curricular pattern the child is experiencing in school. It is considered that the teachers in each classroom are so committed to their particular curriculum procedures that they can implement them in home teaching sessions.

The three curricular orientations utilized for work with children at the time of my visit were described under the headings of Language Training, Cognitively Oriented, and Unit Based Curricula. The Language Training Curriculum is patterned after the Bereiter-Engelmann program at the University of Illinois; the Cognitively Oriented Curriculum follows along the lines of that used in the Perry Preschool Program with a Piagetian focus; the Unit Based Curriculum is the one they call "traditional" nursery education. I spent brief periods of time in the classrooms with the first two curricular orientations. A visit to what was considered the more traditional program could not be readily facilitated. Weikart described the traditional nursery school methods as maturationally oriented; watching and waiting for needs to emerge and timing activities to this emergence. He designated the goals as social, emotional, and motor development(76).

The Language Training program took place in the afternoon in the same classroom where different children had had more materials to utilize in the Cognitively Oriented morning program. All enticing equipment was turned to the wall and effectively barricaded so that children had no access to it. The language "lesson" centered first around direct teaching of the term "building." It was defined as "something you can walk into." Then the teacher asked "Can I fool you? Which of these are buildings—barn, house, store, eraser?" The reading "lesson" centered upon developing an ability to sound out words. The first exercise consisted of the teacher overemphasizing and extending sounds with directions to the child to "say it fast." For example:

m . . . . . . e . . . . . say it fast me
i . . . . . . f . . . . . say it fast if
a . . . . . dd . . . . . say it fast add
a . . . . . . m . . . . . say it fast am

The next exercise reversed the process.

The word is seed. say it slowly s e e e e d d.
The word is rid. say it slowly r i i i i d d.
The word is is. say it slowly i i i i i s s.

Direct verbal input plus supposed "simplification" of processes related to skill development prevailed.

The Cognitively Oriented Curriculum has such intellectual goals as the understanding of and responding to temporal relations (beginning and end, ordering of events); and the understanding of and use of classifications (gross conceptual discriminations, descriptive classifications of size, shape and color). To support an understanding of temporal relations, at the end of the morning children gathered together in a group to recall the day's events. It was largely the teacher who recalled how the day began, what came next, how it would end, and finally projected the activities of the next day.

During part of my observation in this classroom, the children were grouped for the learning of classification by size, shape, color, and quantity. I have already described the experience the youngest group had discussing the fruit and candy corn they had previously purchased at the supermarket. In my earlier discussion, I pointed out the negative emotional residues of this period which, in my estimation, far outweighed any cognitive gains. Of course, I don't believe the researchers have any intention of building feelings of guilt or deprivation. Perhaps it is that a program, so obviously emphasizing cognitive gains, turns teachers away from awareness of affective dimensions, so that they become oblivious to the real meaning of an experience for young children. Or does the difference lie not so much in *what* the teacher does, but *how* she does it? In this case, teacher style of operation is more important than "curricula style." If the latter is true, and I believe it holds great significance for the facilitation of learning, for the planning of research projects, and for the evaluation of child growth, then this project is ignoring a most significant variable.

Weikart's interest in intervention programs and their equivocal preliminary results have led him to question basic issues. He speculates that schools may be attacking "the wrong problem with the wrong person"(77). The mother's childrearing practices may need to be the focus. As with others, his work with three- and four-year-olds turns him to the very young child and his home.

Early Childhood Language Project— University of California, Los Angeles

An example of projects with a single focus is the Early Childhood Language Project directed by Dr. Carolyn Stern. That the child's language must conform to the expectations of the school system and become elaborated enough to aid in problem solving is a major premise of this program(78). The program proposes to alter the language of the disadvantaged child while he is very young, so that it may conform to the language of the school. Two years of language lessons are given to children at the ages of three and four. Children already enrolled in day care centers are taken from their classrooms for a fifteen-minute segment of their day. In the fall of 1967, four groups of children in separate day care centers were included in the project; three groups of children were Negro, one group was Caucasian.

Carefully structured language lessons are designed to compensate for measured areas of language deficiency. While the material is not on a machine, it is programmed. There is a laboratory where the structured lessons are developed. Art students plan visual materials. In the taping lab much of the material which comes over headsets is set out in programmed sequences. Materials are made to be self-teaching. A warm, responsive personality is the only requirement for those who administer the materials. Non-trained persons are trained as they go from lesson to lesson.

The first set of programmed material focuses upon the language of instruction and is oriented to looking, listening, and responding. A linguistic bias dominates much of the material. Child response and feedback are built into the sequences. For example, responses to some pictures are to be found in dots impregnated with red or green coloring. With a water pen the children touch the dots; green responses are correct.

Pre- and post-tests have been administered to experimental populations and controls and to children with varying socio-economic backgrounds. Tests for visual and auditory discrimination and for measurement of the child's expressive vocabulary have been developed in the project. Post-test results show substantial language growth. No other aspects of growth are included in this project except references to the child's concept of self. Here, the underlying assumption holds that when you build competence you automatically build self-esteem.

Evaluation in Preschool Programs

Dilemmas in the objective evaluation of innovative programs are many. The kinds of paper and pencil tests and scales frequently used to test program effectiveness omit significant areas of growth. Gains in factual knowledge are the most readily measured. Affective growth—positive or negative—joy in learning or generalized guilt—these are the difficult areas to measure, yet most significant for the total growth of the individual. The fact is that some of the least significant gains are most readily evaluated, while the most significant long-range life gains are so elusive they almost defy precise measurement techniques. Of the affective realm Bloom writes, "This has been a difficult area to measure and one is struck by the lack of a unified view about how to measure these characteristics and the general lack of instruments which are regarded as clearly valid and useful by workers in the field"(79).

Bloom also raises the problems related to the measurements of a specific characteristic at a point in time, and the relationship of this characteristic to the environment in which the child has lived prior to this time(80). Large inferential leaps are generally made between test results and environmental causative factors. Unless researchers begin to build measures which look at varied and complex environmental factors and authenticate a relationship between these factors and the development of characteristics, one needs to look skeptically at comparative research.

Consider these statements by Bloom:

> By environment, we mean the conditions, forces, and external stimuli which impinge upon the individual. These may be physical, social as well as intellectual forces and conditions. . . . We regard the environment as providing a network of forces and factors which surround, engulf, and play on the individual . . . . If we think of environment as giving opportunities for interaction and experience, it may be contended that no two individuals have had the same interactions and experiences. . . . We believe it to be possible to find ways of describing and measuring environments as they affect and, to some extent, determine particular human characteristics. . . . However, the environmental measure must include more than the availability of a supply of such elements and care; it must also determine the extent to which they are utilized by the individuals under study" (81).

These statements point up the complexity of comparative studies. How can he expect to demonstrate the "assets" of various programs when we lack the necessary measures Bloom designates? By ignoring significant variables, by failing to relate measurement to the total spectrum necessary for meaningful results, findings may be more than spurious; they may lead people who enter into early childhood education grossly astray.

Some research projects are searching for more valid and more varied measures of the growth of young children. Better measurement devices may result from the increased attention to early childhood.

Notes

[1]Mary B. Lane, *Abstract of Research Project* (San Francisco State College, Mimeo, n.d.), p. 1.

[2]Mary B. Lane, *Educational and Mental Health Consequences of a Nursery School Program in a Cross Cultural Setting* (San Francisco State College, Mimeo, n.d.), pp. 4-5.

[3]Mary B. Lane, *Nurseries in Cross-Cultural Education* (San Francisco State College, Pamphlet, n.d.), p. 4.

[4]Mary B. Lane, *Educational and Mental Health Consequences,* p. 10.

[5]*Ibid.*

[6]Mary B. Lane, *Abstract,* p. 3.

[7]Mary B. Lane, *Educational and Mental Health Consequences,* p. 11.

[8]Mary B. Lane, "The Young Child: Priorities and Potentials," *Young Children,* XXII (March, 1967), p. 223.

[9]*Ibid.,* p. 224.

[10]From notes taken while reading an original proposal for the project.

[11]*Preliminary Review* (Early Childhood Center, Bank Street College of Education, Mimeo, March 30, 1966), p. 2.

[12]*Ibid.,* p. 20.

[13]*Ibid.,* p. 24.

[14]Jane Wagner, *Mrs. Remo's Living Room* (New York: Bank Street College of Education, March, 1967), p. 1.

[15]*Preliminary Review,* p. 6.

[16]Hanna Sonquist, Constance Kamii, and Louise Derman, *A Piaget-Derived Curriculum,* Ypsilanti, Michigan Public Schools, Mimeo, August, 1968, p. 1.

[17]*Ibid:*

[18]Constance Kamii and Louise Derman, *The Development of a Piaget-Derived Curriculum and a Model for Introducing a New Curriculum in a Public-School Setting,* Ypsilanti Public Schools, Mimeo, March, 1969, p. 6.

[19]*Ibid.*

[20]Constance K. Kamii and Norma L. Radin, *A Framework for a Pre-*

school Curriculum, Ypsilanti Public Schools, Mimeo, July, 1968, p. 4. (This is part of a forthcoming book, in press.)

[21]*Ibid.*, p. 9.

[22]*Ibid.*, p. 10.

[23]Hanna Sonquist and Constance Kamii, "Applying Some Piagetian Concepts in the Classroom for the Disadvantaged," *Young Children,* XXII (March, 1967), p. 233.

[24]Sonquist, Kamii, and Derman, *A Piaget-Derived Curriculum,* p. 12.

[25]*Ibid.*, p. 14.

[26]Frank G. Jennings, "Jean Piaget: Notes on Learning," *Saturday Review* (May 20, 1967), p. 83.

[27]Sonquist, Kamii, and Derman, *A Piaget-Derived Curriculum,* p. 15.

[28]Millie Almy, *et al., Young Children's Thinking* (New York: Teachers College Press, 1966), p. 135.

[29]Kamii and Derman, . . . *A Model for Introducing a New Curriculum,* p. 4.

[30]Glorianne Wittes, *A Parent Education Program for 1968–1969,* Ypsilanti Public Schools, Mimeo, March, 1969, p. 1.

[31]*Ibid.*, p. 2.

[32]Carolyn Plummer, *The Home-Visit Program,* Ypsilanti Public Schools, Mimeo, March, 1969, p. 1.

[33]*Handbook: Early Childhood Education,* Berkeley, California: Berkeley Unified School District, 1967-1968, unpaged.

[34]"Bing Nursery School," *Childhood Education,* 45 (May, 1969), pp. 513-516.

[35]Philip W. Jackson and Bernice J. Wolfson, "Varieties of Constraint in Nursery School," *Young Children,* XXIII (September, 1968), p. 359.

[36]*Ibid.*, p. 367.

[37]James D. Koerner, "EDC: General Motors of Curriculum Reform," *Saturday Review* (August 19, 1967), pp. 56-58.

[38]Arthur L. Singer, Jr., "Report from the President," *Education Development Center Annual Report 1967* (Newton, Massachusetts: Education Development Center, 1967), pp. 13-14.

[39]Allan Leitman, "Early Childhood Education Study," *Education Development Center Annual Report 1967* (Newton, Massachusetts: Education Development Center, 1967), p. 43.

[40]Allan Leitman, *Space for Teachers* (Newton, Massachusetts: Education Development Center, 1968), Mimeo, p. 1.

[41]Allan Leitman, *Ethological Films in Education* (Newton, Massachusetts: Education Development Center, 1968), Mimeo, p. 1.

[42]*Ibid.*, p. 3.

[43]*They Can Do It*, Film Library, Education Development Center, Newton, Massachusetts.

[44]Allan Leitman and Cornelia Voorhees, *Moments in Learning* (Newton, Massachusetts: Early Childhood Education Study, Education Development Center, n.d.).

[45]*Single Sheets* (Newton, Massachusetts: Early Childhood Education Study, Education Development Center, n.d.).

[46]*Making Things to Learn*, Film Library, Education Development Center, Newton, Massachusetts.

[47]Cynthia P. Deutsch and Martin Deutsch, "Brief Reflections on the Theory of Early Childhood Enrichment Programs," in *The Disadvantaged Child: Selected Papers of Martin Deutsch and Associates* (New York: Basic Books, 1967), p. 381.

[48]For an explanation see Martin Whiteman, Bert R. Brown, and Martin Deutsch, "Some Effects of Social Class and Race on Children's Language and Intellectual Abilities, in *The Disadvantaged Child* (New York: Basic Books, 1967), pp. 319-335.

[49]Martin Deutsch and Bert R. Brown, "Social Influences in Negro-White Intelligence Differences," in *The Disadvantaged Child* (New York: Basic Books, 1967), p. 306.

[50]Deutsch and Deutsch, *The Disadvantaged Child,* p. 384.

[51]Martin Deutsch, "Early Social Environment and School Adaptation," in *The Disadvantaged Child* (New York: Basic Books, 1967), p. 139.

[52]Lassar G. Gotkin, "A Calendar Curriculum for Disadvantaged Kindergarten Children," *Teachers College Record,* LXVIII (February, 1967), p. 406.

[53]Lassar G. Gotkin and Fay Fondiller, "Listening Centers in the Kindergarten," *Audiovisual Instruction,* 10 (January, 1965), p. 26.

[54]Martin Deutsch, "Early Social Environment and School Adaptation," in *The Disadvantaged Child* (New York: Basic Books, 1967), p. 140.

[55]Carl Bereiter, *et al.*, "An Academically Oriented Pre-School for Culturally Deprived Children," in *Pre-School Education Today,* ed. Fred M. Hechinger (Garden City, New York: Doubleday, 1966), p. 106.

[56]Wesley Becker and Siegfried Engelmann, "University of Illinois Program," *Some New Approaches in Early Childhood Education.* Material distributed by Head Start at the Head Start Conference in Houston, Texas, December, 1968, Mimeo, p. 2. (Carl Bereiter left the program in 1966. Later Wesley Becker became associated with it.)

[57]Carl Bereiter and Siegfried Engelmann, *Teaching Disadvantaged Children in the Preschool* (Englewood Cliffs, New Jersey: Prentice-Hall, 1966), p. 87.

[58]*Ibid.*, pp. 54-56.

[59]Constance Kamii and Louise Derman, *The Englemann Approach to Teaching Logical Thinking: Findings from the Administration of Some Piagetian Tasks,* Ypsilanti, Michigan: Ypsilanti Public Schools, Mimeo, February, 1969, pp. 16, 18, 19-20, 22. (Part of book in press.)

[60]William E. Martin, "Rediscovering the Mind of the Child: A Significant Trend in Research in Child Development," *Merrill-Palmer Quarterly,* 6 (January, 1960), p. 73.

[61]*The Reinforcement Sequence*, Syracuse, New York: Center for Research and Development in Early Childhood Education, Syracuse University, Mimeo, p. 1.

[62]*Telling Time,* Syracuse, New York: Center for Research and Development in Early Childhood Education, Syracuse University, Mimeo, p. 1.

[63]William J. Meyer, *Quarterly Progress Report,* Submitted to the National Laboratory on Early Childhood Education about the Center for Research and Development in Early Childhood Education, Syracuse University, March 15, 1968, Mimeo, p. 3.

[64]Laura Dittman, ed., "An Interview with Glen Nimnicht," *Young Children,* XXIII (March, 1968), p. 212.

[65]Glen Nimnicht, *et al., Progress Report on Research at the New Nursery School* (Greeley, Colorado: Colorado State College, 1967), Mimeo, p. 5.

[66]*Ibid.,* pp. 5-6.

[67]*Ibid.*, p. 7.

[68]Glen Nimnicht, "The Autotelic-Discovery Approach," *Some New Approaches in Early Childhood Education.* Material distributed by Head Start at the Head Start Conference in Houston, Texas, December, 1968, Mimeo, p. 1.

[69]Oralee McAfee, "The Right Word," *Young Children,* XXIII (November, 1967), p. 78.

[70]Kenneth D. Wann and Helen F. Robison, "Summary," *Study of Intellectual Stimulation of Disadvantaged Pre-Kindergarten Children, Sponsored by Center for Urban Education, New York City.* Teachers College, Columbia University, Department of Curriculum and Teaching, June 30, 1967, Mimeo, p. 1.

[71]David P. Weikart, *Preliminary Results from a Longitudinal Study of Disadvantaged Preschool Children.* Paper presented at the 1967 convention of the Council for Exceptional Children, Mimeo, pp. 3-4.

[72]*Ibid,* p. 2.

[73]*Ibid.* p. 5.

[74]David P. Weikart, *Application for Ypsilanti Preschool Curriculum Demonstration Project*, To be funded under Title III of the Elementary and Secondary Education Act. Ypsilanti Public Schools, June 30, 1967, Mimeo, p. 4.

[75]*Ibid.,* p. 16.

[76]David P. Weikart, "Preschool Programs: Preliminary Findings," *Journal of Special Education,* I (Winter, 1967), p. 165.

[77]David P. Weikart and Dolores Z. Lambie, *Preschool Intervention Through a Home Teaching Project.* Paper presented at the 1968 convention of the American Educational Research Association, Mimeo, p. 2.

[78]Carolyn Stern, "Language Competencies of Young Children," *Young Children,* XXII (October, 1966), p. 45.

[79]Benjamin S. Bloom, *Stability and Change in Human Characteristics* (New York: Wiley, 1964), p. 133.

[80]*Ibid.,* pp. 9-10.

[81]*Ibid.,* pp. 187-188.

Programs for Children in the Primary Grades

Probably the most significant, promising, and far-reaching change at the primary level relates to a reorganization of a school and/or a classroom to promote individualized learning. This change, when logically carried out, reaches every aspect of the curriculum—the teacher, the motivations for learning, and, necessarily, what is learned. It is frequently accompanied by a revitalization of curriculum and a strengthened bond between the world of the classroom and the world outside.

New Patterns of Organization

The traditional one grade for one age level, the mode or organization that has dominated elementary schools for over a century, developed in response to a demand to make schools "efficient" promoters of learning. It was under this pattern of organization that teaching took on the fallacious position that lessons should be geared to the child of "average ability." Not only did teachers fail to reach many children of varying ability on either end of the continuum, but many children categorized as "average" could not accommodate their learning to a single-content, single-methodology, single-answer approach to education. Age is only one determinant of growing powers and an exceedingly fallible means of building a single curriculum for all children. Instead, we need to look at a host of other factors which make each child a unique person.

World of Inquiry— Rochester, New York

One example of extensive reorganization is a school already referred to: the World of Inquiry, located in Rochester, New York. This school represents a departure from the traditional age-grade structure. Here, children of mixed age levels (five- to seven-year-olds together, or larger age-range groupings) have as their home base a "family room" where reading and social studies form the core of the learning experiences for individuals and small groups. Centers have been developed in various areas of the school for other aspects of the curriculum such as mathematics, science, and the creative arts where children can pursue projects of personal relevancy. Great flexibility for individual and small-group learning is provided by this total school organization. Individual inquiry is indeed promoted. Children have an abundance of free choice of activity and move at their own pace with a great deal of individualized attention. One teacher reported, "In public schools I saw kids held back by the system. You couldn't take them as far and as fast as they could go. Here, that's our whole purpose. This is where the action is."

The area designed for the creative arts is ingeniously arranged for varying, concurrent projects—from creative dramatics, clay modeling, and painting to cooking. On the occasion of my visit a small group was cooking while a number of individual children were working with various art media. Each child in the school has a large drawer in which to keep his work. Circular folding partitions in the center of the room can be closed when a small group wishes to be involved in creative dramatics. At times, one end can be opened to accommodate an audience. This arrangement in the middle of the room helps to set up areas, somewhat separated, for other artistic endeavors.

Inner- and outer-city pupils mingle in the School of Inquiry. The careful integration of classrooms has gained publicity for the school as a model, futuristic, integrated one. Children are selected to represent a cross section of Rochester's economic and racial makeup. The school, situated in the inner-city, is drawing white children from the outer-city. Indeed, many more white parents, as well as black parents, wished to enroll their children in the school than it could possibly accommodate. To build up this reverse flow into an inner-city school is a noteworthy achievement.

Whatever content is selected for social study in the various family rooms, social learnings grow daily, for racial understandings expand as children work together. One Negro boy proudly stated, "We don't have any enemies in this school." A white ten-year-old commented, "You learn that some Negroes are nice and some aren't. And that's the way it is with whites; and that's the way it is with anything else"(1).

Cooperative Project—University of Arizona and Tucson District No. 1

The organization of the classroom to promote responsive adult-child relationships and to provide for small, vital learning groups is one prominent feature of the program for children developed and directed out of the Early Childhood Education Laboratory at the University of Arizona. This is flexible organization at the classroom level, for the children of the project are enrolled in first, second and third grades of Tucson elementary schools. The schools selected for the project are those with the largest proportion of economically limited families. In this geographical location, most of the families are Mexican-American. Dr. Marie Hughes, director of the project, describes many of the children as underdeveloped, as lacking in the experiences which will build the abilities and cognitive processes prevalent in middle-class children(2). Children from these families have, in the past, found school irrelevant and meaningless for them, have reacted with a general passivity to school tasks, and have become early school dropouts. The program is designed to counteract these unfortunate developments. Thus, the classroom has been organized so that responsive one-to-one relationships are augmented, and frequently changing, small learning groups are made possible; each holding the potential for building positive attitudes toward achievement.

Rooms are arranged with interest centers to maximize the child's interactions with materials, adults, peers. In commenting upon Piaget's theories and Hunt's emphasis upon the importance of the child's transactions with his environment, Marie Hughes writes, "If interaction with the environment is of such importance in the development of the child, then the nature of that environment, social and physical, becomes of concern to all who wish children to grow into their full potential"(3). Careful thought is given to each environmental component. Classrooms have heterogeneous groups of children in order to increase opportunities to learn from peer models. Adults work with children in small groups so that teachers can "respond to each individual child, utilize his current skills, and build upon and extend this base"(4). Materials are abundant to provide choice and, at the same time, to foster important social and intellectual skills. Structure is present in committee work and certain designated tasks, but great flexibility is possible in their fulfillment.

The goals of the program are extensive and long-range. They include the development of language competence, an intellectual base, a motivational base, and societal arts and skills. The extended use of linguistic labels is only one of the language skills considered. Others include concept building and an awareness of the function of language. Intellectual base skills include such things as ordering and sequencing, but also the ability to organize one's behavior toward a goal or to evaluate alternatives. A positive attitude toward learning and an expectation of success rank high among motivational considerations. Societal arts and skills include not only the traditional ones of reading, writing, and arithmetic, but the social skills of cooperation and planning together(5). The program is "orchestrated" so that goals are not isolated or skills taught separately. Skills are developed functionally, thus allowing for more than one to be developed simultaneously. The functionality of the learning settings also promotes transfer into the life of the child both in school and out of it.

Most of my time in Tucson was spent in the primary classrooms of three of the project schools. I was impressed with the richness of life experience available. All efforts are made to help children to an awareness of their environment and to make this an integral part of learning experiences. Many trips are taken with the rule of thumb being two walks to one bus trip so that all the possibilities of the immediate neighborhood are exploited for learning. At the time of my visit in the spring of 1968, rooms exuded evidence of the variety and meaning of these experiences for children. The trips, plus a wealth of follow-up and expanded classroom activities, formed the natural setting for language growth. Many of the children are from Spanish speaking homes and have a limited ability to speak English. The free-flowing activities of the classroom formed situations requiring a rich interplay of language, where English was spoken consistently.

In one first-grade classroom, the children were described as ninety per cent Mexican-American and as non-verbal, withdrawn, and shy when they entered school the past September. As I entered the classroom, a busy hum, including extensive verbal interchange, prevailed. The children were working individually or in small groups with a variety of self-selected equipment—blocks, paint, housekeeping equipment, a feel box, tapes and earphones, picture dictionaries and other books. Some children were making shape books—stories they had written or dictated appropriate to the shape they had made, such as a mouse or a bunny. One of their bulletin boards was "All About a Mouse," employing such words as tiny, teeny, skinny, tall, and giant.

In a corner of another room was an attractively arranged bulletin board with the expressions of children, part of which said:

> Michael said, "It is not a bone."
>
> Richard said, "It is a bone.
> It has meat on it.
> It's all hard. It's a
> little bit cold."
>
> "Smells like a banana."
>
> "It's crooked."
>
> "It has juice."
>
> "It looks like a
> red stick."
>
> "It's something to
> make salad."
>
> "It's red celery."

Beside this was a recipe for rhubarb sauce which the children had made and eaten after the discussion. In such an experience multiple learnings grow: vocabulary extensions, new concepts, the sequencing of events, intellectual and social skills.

In this same first grade, the children had selected three stories: "The Six Foolish Fishermen," "The Three Pigs," and "The Little Red Hen." Three committees met at varying times to prepare some kind of presentation to the rest of the class. One committee had chosen to present their story through puppets. Another group was planning to make costumes for their dramatization. Meaningful oral language growth was accompanied by improved social cooperation skills, by conceptual growth, and by growth in self-direction.

Another class took a walk to a nearby parking lot. When they returned, committees put together a collage of the things they had found there and wrote stories about them. A bulletin board called

"A Touching Walk" displayed the results. For example, one group collected a cattail, a feather, a leaf, a stick, and a crumpled can and wrote:

> We found 3 long things.
> Two are hard.
> One is soft.
> A leaf is crunchy.
> A can is made out of metal. It's cold, hard and bumpy.

Such experiences formed the usual procedure of every classroom. Cooking, tasting, visiting, walking, and feeling provided the foundation for meaty, eloquent oral and written expression which gained in form and substance with somewhat older children.

The project has been going long enough for the first group of children to have nearly completed the third grade(6). These children were doing well on standardized tests of language ability—one traditional measure of the effectiveness of the program. Language skills were gained meaningfully and purposefully.

While a major emphasis is one of confrontation of the in-school and out-of-school environment, it is not expected that this alone will build the wide range of intellectual abilities necessary in today's society. Dr. Hughes believes there is a lot of work to be done in bridging from the concrete to the abstract. Children need help in this bridging. Concept building, labeling, and recall form the basis for higher levels of abstractions. Experimental, semi-structured lessons have been designed for the teacher to use with a small group of children (five or fewer) to provide for them the opportunity to acquire and practice a range of cognitive processes including those of labeling, recall, categorization, and differentiation. Through open-ended questioning, the process of abstraction is encouraged. This seems to be a most promising direction—one of the few uniquely new concepts of supporting children's cognitive growth.

Let us look at an example of this kind of experience in the classroom. On one of the days of my visit a program assistant was in the classroom with four children using a collection, "a kit," of hinges, including scissors, tweezers, a door hinge, a spring clothes pin, glasses frames, a bow tie clip, and others. The hinges had been in the room for some time for free investigation and manipulation. Now, the program assistant was helping the children to recall, differentiate, and project. She asked, "Have you seen anything like this before (recall)?" They discussed the differences in size and shape (differentiation). They compared the things that hinges are like and not like (generalization). They were asked "How would you use it (projection)?" When the active discussion waned somewhat, the children were asked to find something in the room that "worked in the same way." It proved a good way to check their comprehension. They pointed to door hinges, one on a desk top that lifted, a box that had a lid with a hinge, etc. But one girl came back with a paste jar. When asked about it she said it was a hinge because it would open and shut. And so they investigated hinges more closely to find what specifically differentiated them.

A staff of consultants, called "program assistants," from the Early Childhood Education Laboratory work with teachers and with children in these public school classrooms. Indeed, the extent of the cooperation between the public schools and this component of the National Laboratory of Early Childhood Education is outstanding. The program assistants are really change agents, introducing and maintaining the program's innovative practices in the classrooms. They communicate new techniques to the teacher largely through demonstration. But they also assist the teacher in planning, obtaining materials, and coordinating activities. The recommended ratio of program assistants to teachers in initial stages of program implementation is one-to-five(7).

Not only is this program effective and appropriate for young children, but it is set in the context of significant long-range goals. While new emphasis is given to cognitive growth, all aspects of growth are considered and planned for. The knowledgeable and ingenious leadership in the program promises to add to our knowledge of young children in a manner that should have extensive impact. A strong staff has been drawn to the project. The teachers in the schools were unanimous in their praise—extolling what they have gained in their ability to improve children's learning and to help them to optimal personal functioning.

Learning to Learn Program—Jacksonville, Florida

Based upon the increasingly familiar premise that the major objective of education is to help the child learn how to learn is the school in Jacksonville, Florida directed by Herbert Sprigle. In order to assist the child to be a self-propelling learner, Sprigle believes that learning must be alive and sufficiently meaningful to pose a challenge to him, to spark his curiosity, as well as to provide internal satisfaction and feelings of adequacy. This is a stiff demand if it is interpreted individually for each child, but it represents a big step forward in primary education. Basic tenets of the program include the child as an active participant, immediate usefulness of learning so that it becomes a permanent part of the child's repertoire, feedback that the knowledge gained makes a contribution to himself and others, and multiple sensory and motor activities. It is considered that "the timing, continuity, and structuring of learning experiences are more important than the simple exposure to them"(8).

I was kindly given the permission to visit the program, even though the circumstances for keeping it going were temporarily difficult. In 1967–68, two groups were operating; one was for fours, the other for sixes. The six-year-olds were housed in a public school classroom, the four-year-olds in the converted home called the Learning to Learn School. But the teacher's strike was in full force in Florida, and in order to keep the six-year-old group going it had just been moved into the private building and the children were adjusting to their new surroundings. The day I am about to describe may not have been very typical for this program with its emphasis upon exposures to multiple sensorimotor activities and the process of problem solving. For the problems on the morning of my observation were always those set by the teacher, with no learner involvement in defining the task and setting about to find ways to solve it. Also, the viewing booth was not equipped with sound and parts of the room were not visible.

The first task the children were given was to write a story. They had recently acquired two new fish for the classroom. The children were asked to put themselves in the place of the fish and answer the questions: "Why are these children here? What are they doing?" The teacher put words on the board to help them; they used picture dictionaries; they utilized their own individual word cards; children helped each other. And the stories were written. The teacher reported later that the stories were not as good as the children usually created. The questions were hard for them. It was difficult for them to see things through the eyes of another; it was difficult for them to interpret school activities. Next, children were given three individual assignments to complete during the morning in whatever order they chose and at their own speed. Some were working at a typewriter; some were receiving directions from a tape recorder with earphones; others were employed with all kinds of games. The teacher and a student teacher used reading games with small groups of children.

This program is freeing children physically and socially, giving them freedom to set their own timetable for the tasks given them. Many tasks were presented in a game setting which the children enjoy.

At the end of the morning session, each child was given a learning game to take home to play with his parents over the weekend. This is considered a serious responsibility of the child and his parents and is indicative of steps taken to help parents understand the program. As the director forcefully states, "One place to start the crusade for better schools and quality education is to educate the parents as you educate the child"(9). There is no doubt that one of the crying needs in education today is to help parents understand the educational myths that undergird programs in many traditional primary classrooms, and to help them see the directions of educational change which will provide more meaningful education for their children.

Herbert Sprigle is obviously reaching many of the parents of children in the project. Throughout the time children were enrolled, monthly discussion groups were held for parents. Groups were kept small in the interest of active discussion. These group meetings, plus conferences, classroom observation, and home participation with children have made the parents great supporters of the program. At the time of my visit, the six-year-old group had been together as fives the year before with no plans to continue the program for them. The parents initiated the idea that the children remain together in first grade and go on with the same kind of program. This was done and the parents cooperated even though the site obtained made travel distances great for some of them. The parents requested that monthly meetings be continued. The effectiveness of the parent program is encouraging.

The five-year-old program had been put within a research framework by matching groups each selected "from lower-middle socio-economic class families whose parents had a high school education or less." Two control groups of twenty-three children were included: one which remained at home and had no formal preschool training and one enrolled in a kindergarten in the community. The pre- and post-testing included measures of motor coordination, tests of general intelligence and reasoning ability, and tests of expressive abilities(10). The results favor the Learning How to Learn Program, with differences most apparent in language skills—especially story telling.

University Elementary School—
University of California, Los Angeles

Famous for the application of ideas of non-grading is the University Elementary School in Los Angeles. The directors, past and present, John Goodlad and Madeline Hunter, contend that the school is characterized by four big ideas: non-grading, team teaching, individual diagnosis and prescription, and defining objectives in behavioral terms. The school, of course, is a campus school enrolling children with as varied a background as possible considering its location in a highly affluent section of Los Angeles. The purpose of the school is inquiry into promising ideas related to educational theory and practice.

The directors think of their school as four broad phases with function and expectation overlapping: an early childhood level, a lower elementary phase, a middle and upper elementary level. The early childhood level for three-, four-, five-, and six-year-olds has four basic objectives—that each child:

1. Become a human being in his own right—develop a sense of autonomy.
2. Learn to work and play productively with his peers.
3. Work productively with ideas and materials.
4. Relate appropriately to adults.

When a child has attained these objectives, he is ready for the lower elementary phase of the school. The administration and faculty say they do not worry whether five- and six-year-olds have an interest in reading, though many of them are reading.

In the lower elementary phase (roughly ages six to eight or nine) there is a continuing concern for self-concept plus a major emphasis upon the development of the fundamental skills—especially reading. If a seven-year-old is not progressing in reading, efforts are made to help the child succeed. At the middle elementary (ages seven to ten) and upper elementary (ages nine to twelve) levels four objectives are listed:

1. Learn to evaluate himself.
2. Develop strategies for learning a given task.
3. Develop a zest for learning.
4. Increasingly be self-propelling in learning(11).

These are not considered to be organizational units of the school, as some clusters of children cut across the age spans, but they are emphasized as indicating that an elementary school is not unitary throughout but is subject to shifts in emphasis.

The concept of diagnosis and prescription enters into the formulation of the non-graded groups. Two questions are prominent in deciding the specific group for the specific child: What kind of teacher does this child need at this moment in time? What kind of peer groups should he have? Teachers are viewed as differing on three dimensions: 1) their style (warm and nurturing or demanding and staccato), 2) the predictability of their environment (an organized classroom or one that allows great freedom), and 3) the size of learning steps taken (slow, steady progression or big learning bites). In the spring, the fall groupings are made with careful consideration of the teacher characteristics which will foster learning for each child, though the job of the teacher may be to wean a child from an overwhelming need at one period of time. The development of leadership abilities is a consideration in diagnosing the kind of a peer group the child should have. If, for example, a child has been a ready leader in one group, he may be put into a cluster where he has to work for a leadership role. The interesting fact is that in forming clusters, academic achievement, the one standard that dominated grade levels, is not prominent. The directors consider that a non-graded school does not exist if groups are made on the basis of achievement, that teaching levels can be manipulated more readily than other factors.

The fallacy of grade-level progression became obvious to teachers as they looked at the wide range of interests, abilities, and aptitudes in children all of the same age. But the move to non-grading and diagnosis and prescription made some teachers apprehensive. It "began with a few teachers who volunteered to explore the possibilities. Their enthusiastic endorsement encouraged others to venture into the new level of professionalism. At the end of two years the University Elementary School had completed a metamorphosis from a traditional graded school into an educational environment designed to optimize each child's progress"(12).

A limited number of classrooms are self-contained, but most clusters of children work with two or more teachers—a teaching team with the responsibility for the total school experiences of that cluster of children. The team of teachers plan together, teach together, evaluate together. Madeline Hunter proposed that the rigor in team teaching comes through defining objectives; the purpose of the lesson determines the sub-grouping(13). For example, in a cluster of children concerned with measurement in mathematics and dealing with the basic idea that things are measured in man-made units, three sub-groups may be formed in this manner:

Children working with linear measure.	Children working with cubic measure.	Children ready to create a new measure.

Another example was given in social studies related to the development of study skills:

Children learning to contribute.	Children learning to build on the ideas of others.	Children learning to summarize, to extrapolate.

The children for each group are determined through diagnosis and prescription. Thus, after a major objective has been determined, groups are formed to work at various levels for which sub-goals are delineated. Groups do not change every day but are considered to be very flexible.

Behavioral objectives are designated by Madeline Hunter as the means of building precision into teaching, for she believes they enable teachers to select better learning experiences while providing a basis for evaluation(14). She realizes that the easiest things to define in behavioral objectives are the least significant parts of learning—"the rinky-dink things"—and that the more complex the situation, the more difficult the behavioral objectives are to determine. Indeed, experience has shown that written objectives suffer from either being too precise, direct, and limiting, or being so generalized as to give little direction to educational programs and little basis for evaluation. With all the emphasis on teacher diagnosis and prescription and teacher-defined behavioral objectives, one cannot help but raise questions about the role of the learner in the educative process. To what degree can the learner develop a sense of autonomy?

Most of my observations were made at the early childhood level where there was one self-contained classroom, two clusters of three-, four-, and five-year-olds each with a teaching team, and two clusters of four-, five-, and six-year-olds with different teaching teams. Fine physical facilities were available to all. The two clusters of four- to six-year-olds each had a large indoor space and shared a large boat, and a tree house. With the balmy October weather in California and ample running water, almost anything could be done outdoors that could be done indoors: painting, block building, feeding the pets, building at a work bench. The children, most of them outdoors, were engaged in self-directed, self-propelled activities. Much of the morning was available for these self-selected activities with group times for snack, stories, and singing.

One teacher remained inside working with small groups of children in what was called "self-demand reading." As children came by she sent out invitations to join ongoing activities—"Bobby, do you want a turn?" "Alex, have you seen our new book?" A group of about six children played a word game which consisted of categorizing objects whose name began with k, d, or m and putting them in the appropriate sack. An individual child read words that the teacher wrote on the board (at, hat, sat, that; it, hit, sit) and then spent about ten minutes with a pre-primer. Four children came in from outside at 9:25A.M.and asked if it was their reading time. They were accustomed to go with an intern at 9:30A.M.for reading instruction. Is this really self-demand reading? Or are there strong pressures inherent in the environmental situation? Is this linguistic, skill-oriented, fragmented approach consonant with true self-demand? I saw no individual or chart stories which evidenced a desire to work with printed symbols in meaningful ways. The organizational setup did allow for those children who were interested in reading before the age of six to begin. The overwhelming pressures placed on most children to read during the September after their sixth birthday were certainly not there. To this extent the procedure was individualized. But were teachers led by behavioral goals rather than by a bonafide demand by the child?

The six-year-olds in the early childhood area were there because, for some reason, they had not met the designated objectives. For some it was to help them develop leadership abilities by remaining as the oldest in a familiar situation. The decision was not based upon reading ability; all of them could read. It was reported that one child asked one day why he was not with his friends in the lower elementary grouping. He was told he could visit there if he wished. He spent a morning in the other area then willingly rejoined the early childhood group.

Since a chief goal in the lower elementary phase is to build fundamental skills, I was not surprised to see children engaged in reading lessons. There was one self-contained classroom and a large cluster of six-, seven-, and eight-year-olds with a teaching team.

The division of children in rooms and reading experiences is pictured below.

Beginning of the morning:

Teacher and 10 children having difficulty in reading.	Activity Room. 33 children working on own language arts related activities.
Teacher and 23 children reading from reading texts.	Self-contained classroom. 24 children.

Following mid-morning break there was a switch between children in the activity room and those in reading experiences:

Teacher and 15 self-propelled readers—differentiated work.	Activity Room. Other 33 children work on language arts activities.
Teacher and 18 children using reading texts.	Self-contained classroom.

These children were obviously grouped on reading achievement for these periods. It was explained that some of the teachers were new and just beginning to understand the diagnostic process.

In the lower elementary phase, the emphasis on reading skills, as well as on those of writing and mathematics, seemed to diminish a focus on other areas such as social studies. There was no evidence of any rich communion between in-school and out-of-school life to bring vitality to classroom experiences. My observations left me with several unanswered questions. What happens to interpersonal relationships in team teaching? What happens to the sense of community which develops as part of a self-contained classroom? In team teaching, particularly if combined with the concept of diagnosis and prescription, do the teachers do all the decision making? What happens to the goal of individual autonomy under such a regime?

Organizational Change

All of these newer programs have elements of change broader than mere organizational variation, but they all illustrate some degree of organizational shift. The changing of the organizational pattern does not guarantee any change in the teaching-learning process, but it can facilitate or constrain movement toward individualization. Some commitment to non-grading seems to be for the reason of finding a more effective teaching means than group instruction. Whereas a century ago total group instruction on an age-graded basis was viewed as efficient, we now know that this procedure is unequaled for losing and frustrating the largest number of children. As a result some schools are moving toward an organization which offers increased freedom by providing differing amounts of the same experiences and differing rates for achieving goals which are fairly similar for all children. Others are moving toward greater individualization by opening up wider consideration of educational outcomes and by decreasing the emphasis on conformity and putting more emphasis on initiative and independent thinking.

Non-grading, coupled with diagnosis and prescription, while certainly a great advance over age-graded schools, still erects barriers to fostering initiative and individuality in that the teacher needs to make many arbitrary decisions and is tied to a strongly judgmental relationship. It leads the teacher to "focus upon needs, disabilities and problems instead of attending to the pupil as a person who is constantly growing and learning"(15).

In the project at Tucson, some classrooms seemed to provide the greatest opportunity for real choice and independent thinking of any I visited. Here, children helped plan experiences and execute them with self-direction. Much of the living in school was less contrived and more real, thus enabling children to contribute and grow on many levels.

Change in Subject-Matter Areas

Never before in American educational history was a decade so filled with numerous and massive efforts to develop improved content, methods, and materials in specific school subjects as was the sixties. Mathematics, social studies, and science are among the subjects fraught with change. For example, in a three-year period (1962–1965), projects in social studies increased fivefold(16). Furthermore, the early emphasis on secondary school projects was balanced by many including children of elementary school age.

These were extensive and intensive projects funded by foundations or councils and directly involved in curriculum change. These efforts to redefine the role of knowledge in the curriculum have moved away from the former stress upon factual content to stress on the structure of concepts and the principles of inquiry inherent in various fields of knowledge.

Specialists in a subject struggle to keep up with new developments. I could not possibly, during my year's time, delve into any one subject adequately. One project in science drew my attention because not only was its leader reconsidering the nature of science in order to develop a more meaningful program, but he was also looking at the nature of the child. I spent several days at the Science Curriculum Improvement Study at Berkeley, California directed by Robert Karplus. This one study may serve as an example of others.

Science Curriculum Improvement Study — University of California, Berkeley

Robert Karplus is a physicist who became interested in science for young children when he visited the classrooms his children were attending. Appalled at what served as science education in the elementary school, Karplus turned to a consideration of the possibilities and problems of working with children in science. He saw a great discrepancy existing between the concept of science held by scientists and that held by teachers, administrators, and even textbook writers. While scientists view science as "wrestling with problems and apparent contradictions that arise from the observation of natural phenomena"(17), in school it is all too often viewed as the learning of a body of facts or "right answers." To begin with, Professor Karplus planned to place the emphasis upon students' learning through their own observations of science phenomena in the classroom. "He planned also, however, to teach them to interpret their observations in a more analytical way than children do without special instruction. To this end he arranged to teach regularly in a second-grade class at Berkwood School, Berkeley, California"(18). While many science studies were focusing upon the improvement of high school science, Professor Karplus chose to begin at the primary school level where attitudes toward science begin to form.

In developing a new science curriculum, Karplus and the many competent people he had drawn to his staff have been influenced by the theory of Jean Piaget. The elaborations of Piaget's ideas by

Millie Almy, Jerome Bruner, J. McV. Hunt, and Celia Stendler Lavatelli have also governed the program. Some of these people have worked directly with Karplus and his associates. From this school of thought, two related central ideas have been accepted: "1) Children's intellectual capacity passes through a number of qualitatively contrasting states before adulthood. 2) A child's interaction with his environment plays a very significant role in his transition from one stage to the next"(19). Thus, Karplus moves away from reliance on maturational theory to a recognition that intellectual stimulation during the formative years is important in determining the future achievement of each child. He believes that through accumulated experiences children's thinking undergoes a gradual transition from concrete to abstract. Furthermore he writes, "It is . . . the responsibility of the schools to guide the children's development by providing them with particularly informative and suggestive experiences as a base for their abstractions. At the same time, the children must be provided with a conceptual framework that permits them to perceive phenomena in a more meaningful way. This framework will also help them to integrate their inferences into generalizations of greater value than the ones they would form if left to their own devices"(20). Science, he believes, can greatly contribute to this process.

Translated into classroom procedure, this means that science learning must be related to the child's developmental stage; for example, the child should not be asked to reason like an adult until he has attained the stage of formal operations. Science learning also requires the active involvement of the children who perform experiments, make observations, and draw conclusions. Thus, the classroom must become a laboratory. To promote science literacy, the stated goal of this science project, requires that pupils have experiences different from their usual ones—direct experiences (not told or read)—and substantial guidance and discussion to relate these experiences to more usual ones and help build up abstract concepts.

SCIS has developed units based upon a threefold pattern: exploration, invention, and discovery. The core of the unit is the abstraction surrounded by concrete instances and operations. Prior to the introduction of the definition of the abstraction, children engage in several sessions of exploratory experimentation with materials. When they have gone as far as they can on their own, the teacher introduces a key concept to lead them to a new way of thinking about their experiences. This has been called an invention lesson—the introduction of a conceptual invention as a new idea for interpreting experience. The concept is defined as concretely as possible and necessary labels given. The third part of the design, discovery, follows invention as children test the consequences of using the new concept. The distinction between invention and discovery is believed useful in pinpointing those facts that can be discovered and those that cannot.

An example of the teaching strategy may be taken from a unit with young children called *Material Objects*(21). Children readily classify the many objects made available according to size, color, shape, texture. The new idea, the invention, is the concept of "material" as "what it is made of." This not only leads children to classify into categories of wood, metal, rock, etc., but leads them to recognize new relationships between observations and ideas.

The units are developed according to a spiral curriculum concept in which children touch ideas at various levels and the teacher can see what is coming in later years. Much help with the substance and process of science is given to the teacher. The development of one unit involves a long and practical process. The scientists' ideas, with which the units originate, are carefully evaluated by the SCIS staff for the opportunities they offer to challenge children while illustrating key scientific concepts. Exploratory teaching by an SCIS staff member results in the construction of teaching materials, manuals, and equipment kits. This is followed by several classroom trials by teachers and numerous revisions before even preliminary commercial publication is considered. The units are considered to constitute ungraded, sequential physical and life science programs for the elementary school. *Material Objects* is the first physical science unit, followed by others such as *Interaction*, *Relativity*, and *Position and Motion*. *Organisms* is the title of the first unit in the life sciences, followed by others called *Life Cycles*, *Environmental Influences*, and culminating in *Ecosystem* and *Natural Selection*(22).

I observed teachers and children using units in first-, third- and fourth-grade classrooms at Glorietta School, a few miles from the Berkeley campus. In the first grade, the children were working with the *Interaction* unit. The teacher showed the children a pulley system, covered so that they could only see one handle move in response to turning the other. Then each child obtained enough parts to put a pulley together himself. It was interesting to watch them move from random exploration to purposeful assembling of materials. Some children rapidly put the pulley system together and began to link their systems up in a longer chain of pulleys. By the end of the class period, three long linked-up pulley chains had been arranged and children were investigating why some pulleys within the chain operated when the end lever was moved and why some did not. Both enthusiasm and involvement marked the period.

In the third-grade classroom, children were exploring *Relativity* in the use of a reference frame for positioning. The basic concept involved was that position and motion can only be perceived, described, and recognized with reference to other nearby objects. A wooden figure, called Mr. O, was introduced as an omniscient observer, always knowing where other objects were but always describing the location of everything relative to himself. Mr. O was used to report the positioning of a ball, a toy truck, and a wooden block —relative to himself. With great enthusiasm the children reported the positioning of objects from Mr. O's standpoint. One girl had difficulty in doing this until a male visitor lifted her to assume positions similar to those of Mr. O.

By chance, but indicating the spiral curriculum idea, the fourth-graders were engrossed in *Position and Motion*. They were working in groups of three and their equipment included a tripod with a protractor. One child was acting as direction reader, one as pacer, and one as recorder. Given a starting point and a reference point, they were finding the precise dimensions to locate another object. They were practicing in the room using various objects as the reference landmarks and preparing to work out-of-doors the next day.

Teachers and students were enthusiastic about the ideas and materials of this project. A significant and varied science program was underway. But one big question plagued me. How can these ideas and materials be used more flexibly and in an individualized teaching situation? In all the classrooms I visited, the teacher and the whole class were occupied with the science lesson. Indeed, the units have been built to fit the existing school system with group work predominating. Three 30-minute science lessons per week are planned. It is possible to relate the materials to individual differences by the usual means of pacing and adding extra activities for the very fast learning child. But this is not enough. How can the challenging results of this study be utilized in self-propelled, individualized learning? This is a key question. When I raised this question with some project staff members, their response was that they were having a hard enough time getting teachers to free children to really manipulate materials. I know the first-grade teacher was somewhat perturbed by the noise of children putting pulleys together, though it was a most reasonable noise level—that of a busy laboratory. In the hands of a creative teacher, I believe the materials can be used effectively with individuals and small groups.

A wealth of material is available to help teachers become familiar with the project. Trial centers are spread throughout the country which serve not only as locales for evaluating materials developed, but as places where the program can be observed. Center coordinators are located at Teachers College, Columbia University; The University of Hawaii; the University of Oklahoma; the University of Michigan in East Lansing; and the University of California at Los Angeles. The program is used in the laboratory elementary school and, in some cases, the neighboring public schools.

Denver Early Reading Program

While the language arts are not subject areas but skills—competencies relying on borrowed content for their development—specialists have largely been responsible for school programs. Most reading programs utilized in schools have been designed by reading specialists whose ideas have been incorporated into a series of readers, workbooks, and teacher's manuals. Two reading specialists, professors of education at Colorado State College, Paul McKee and M. Lucille Harrison, "provided the detailed program of instruction which constituted the experimental methodology" of the Cooperative Research Project commonly called the Denver Early Reading Program(23).

McKee and Harrison, dropping faith in maturation and embracing the belief that early intellectual growth depends upon environmental stimulation, make the large inferential leap that children are ready at an earlier age for symbolization—those little black marks on paper that stand for words. Furthermore, they emphasize the need to strive to develop readiness and interpret readiness as the mastery of simple skills that undergird higher skills(24).

A seven-step skill program is outlined for kindergarten based on two basic propositions: 1) the importance of context clues in reading and 2) the use of phonic components as the key to unlock words. Therefore, the work focuses upon the ability to use context clues (orally at first) and the growth of visual and auditory discrimination of letters, sounds, and finally words. The seven steps are designated as:

Step	
I	Using spoken context clues.
II	Distinguishing letter forms from one another.
III	Listening for letter sounds.

IV Associating letter sounds and forms.

V Using spoken context and letter-sound association

VI Using spoken context and the first letter in a printed word.

VII Needed practice of the skills listed(25).

Actually, many of these skills were formerly part of reading readiness workbooks used in some kindergartens as designed by specialists. Now the specialists say, "Pencil and paper exercises should usually be avoided, as most kindergarten children will not profit from these activities. Teachers will find a number of games and activities included in this bulletin which can be used to reinforce the skills taught in the seven steps"(26). In Denver they call it an "activity-centered program" and a bold new concept in teaching reading.

I visited seven kindergartens during my stay in Denver. In all but one it was total group teaching with the same types of skill development games in schools in affluent suburban areas as in low-economic, inner-city neighborhoods. Lessons were about twenty minutes long with from twenty-five to thirty-five children sitting and responding to the directions of the teacher. Context sentences were a part of lessons:

In spring a tree is__________. (green, full of leaves).
The sky is__________. (blue, high, dark).

Games for letter recognition were played. For example, children were given letters to hold as they marched around in a circle to music played by the teacher. As the music stopped the teacher called out a letter and the children holding either upper- or lower-case forms of the letter were to hold them high. If they had the letter and did not recognize it they had to sit in the center of the circle. Or a game of sound recognition was played. A number of small objects were placed in front of the teacher: ball, key, fish, rock, barn, ring. The teacher then asked, "Show me something that begins like rain," and the child could pick up the rock or ring.

How does this coincide with what we know about the individual nature of learning? It seems to me that the activities were reinforcing the knowledge of the children who could perform the tasks, but that many children were lost in the process. There was much guessing. In the groups of thirty to thirty-five children some were readily tuning out of the total group activity—learning to get lost in the group. In the light of this observation, my subsequent reading of the following statement by Millie Almy was most meaningful:

> As to specific training for the visual and auditory perception aspects of learning to read, it may be that many of the discriminative abilities that go into the reading process are developed, or fail to develop, long before the child is brought to kindergarten, even prior to nursery school. What goes into the typical reading readiness program at the first grade, or in the kindergarten, may represent for some children too little and too late; and for others, too much and too soon. For example, exercises to facilitate the perception of gross differences may come long after a child has learned to make such distinctions accurately. On the other hand, exercises in noticing subtle differentiations in detail, such as those involved in distinguishing a p from a g, or in maintaining a left-right orientation, may come before a child has had the variety of experiences requisite for the development of such skills. A child who has not achieved "reversibility" in his thought processes and who does not understand reciprocal relationships may lack the stability of perception necessary for formal reading instruction(27).

Here Miss Almy is relating initial instruction in reading to Piagetian theory. It demands a look at individual development rather than a ready acceptance of total group teaching.

The Cooperative Research Project was a five-year project which began in the fall of 1960 "to determine the effectiveness of beginning the systematic teaching of reading in the kindergarten." Groups of children with reading begun in kindergarten were compared to those with reading instruction initiated in first grade. The researchers report that "if pupils who get an early start in reading are kept moving at an optimum rate, they retain the advantages of their early start"(28). The advantages, of course, are measured in terms of norms as evidence of accelerated reading skill. Stimulus-response drill, of which the early skill program consists, will certainly accelerate skill aspects of learning. It places success on verbal skills and the mechanics of word-attack procedures before involvement in reading as a meaningful process.

Can we accept the results of a program only as it affects one aspect of growth? Must we not also look at the way it promotes or at least does not hinder other significant individual goals? As educators, we do want children to read with fluency and understanding. We want them to love reading and to find that it has much to offer them in enriching their lives. We also want them to develop autonomy in learning so that they will become lifelong learners and to realize their highest creative potential. Some research findings of E. Paul Torrance are pertinent here. Among the factors he has found to hinder the development and/or expression of creative thinking are misplaced emphasis on certain verbal skills, expecially on mechanics and on overemphasis on prevention and "success"(29).

Instructional Technology

With the ever increasing technology of our age, teaching machines are proliferating. They cry out for sound considerations of the role they can play in the education of young children. How can they fit into a humanitarian, personalized educative process? As sometimes used today, they dominate a classroom and put subject and sequence before individual potential and continuity. Can they be used to supplement the teacher and to feed into individual growth? Two projects are included here in which educational technology was an integral part of the teaching strategy: the Computer-Assisted Instruction initiated by Patrick Suppes at Stanford University and the Autotelic Responsive Environment designed by Omar Khayyam Moore.

Computer-Assisted Instruction—The Stanford Project

At the Walter Hays School in Palo Alto, I observed students involved in a computer-assisted drill and practice system in mathematics. For no more than seven minutes per day, children came to a room equipped with machines similar to teletype-machines, which each pupil used for individualized practice on computational skills related to the mathematical work of the classroom. As each child sat down at a machine he typed his name and number, and the machine responded with drill exercises based upon his level of performance on the previous day. At the end of each practice sequence the student's performance is automatically evaluated by the computer on the Stanford campus to which the teletype machines are hooked up; then the level of difficulty of the next drill is determined.

In the fall of 1967, two sets of children were using the machines at Walter Hays school: all the fourth-, fifth- and sixth-grade students of the school, and the thirty-two children who remained from a group of forty children selected in 1963 as gifted first-graders. These latter children are in a six-year study of computer-assisted instruction in mathematics. The group I observed were fourth-graders. They came in, immediately proceeded with their seven-minute (or less) practice program, and were oblivious to other children or to me as an observer. The pupil receives immediate feedback step-by-step as he proceeds. At the end, the computer summarizes for him in the following manner: "14 problems with 87 per cent correct in 287 seconds. Goodbye,__________. Please tear off on the dotted line." And each child leaves with his computations immediately corrected and a knowledge of his success for that day.

For the teacher, the computer provides a cumulative history for each student and a record of class growth as follows:

Record of class growth.
Daily status report.
School - Walter Hays
Teacher - Howard
Grade - 04
Class - 02
Time - 1:15 P.M.

The following students are behind and should be encouraged to catch up:

__________ — concept 1
__________ — concept 2

The following students did not run today:

____
____

The average per cent correct for:
concept 1 is 82.

This procedure makes sense. Certain computational skills depend upon some drill and practice in order for automatic response to free the individual to proceed to other levels of mathematical thinking. Great amounts of drudgery are eliminated for both the student and the teacher. Children don't have to copy endless problems from a chalkboard; teachers don't have to check endless numbers of papers. The provision of immediate feedback is helpful in establishing mathematical skills. I had no way of knowing just how closely this drill was related to the on-going mathematics. The individualization no doubt determined the pacing—the level of difficulty

—of the material presented rather than any basic variation in content. The more this type of procedure can be individualized, the more meaningful it will be for learners.

At Brentwood School in East Palo Alto, a much more complex computer-assisted instructional program was in operation. The Stanford CAI was used with four classes enrolling ninety per cent Negro, six per cent Mexican-American, two per cent Oriental-American, and two per cent Caucasian children. The programs with these children were called tutorial with two rooms given a computerized reading program and the others computerized mathematics. At the time of my visit, the three-year reading program was in its second year. The children had been started the previous year as they entered first grade. Teachers of young children will not be surprised that some children had to stop machine instruction until they could learn to follow directions. The classroom teachers also teach reading, and there seems to be little coordination between what they teach and what the computer supplies. It was reported that the Ginn Reading Series is rather generally used by teachers. The CAI is even housed in another building with other adults acting as proctors in the terminal room.

Each child spends between twenty and thirty minutes per day with the computer. As he enters the room, he finds a computer with his name on it, and finds before him equipment for receiving and giving information. He receives messages and information on a picture projector, a cathode-ray tube, and over earphones; he gives answers with a light pen, on a modified typewriter keyboard, or orally.

The reading curriculum was programmed for CAI by a writing team including a linguist, two reading specialists, two psychologists, teachers, and advanced graduate students. Two hundred reading lessons were written early in the work of the program planning and divided into six basic ability levels. The fundamental types of instructional materials include:

1. letter discrimination and identification;
2. initial vocabulary acquisition;
3. word decoding tasks;
4. syntactic and intonation practice with words and phrases;

5. syntactic and semantic practice with phrase and sentence material;

6. information-processing tasks.

An example of a decoding task would be:

```
     an        RR 1:  Touch and say the word that
 r  [   ]             belongs in the empty cell.

    rat        CA:    (Branch to Part D)
    bat
    fan        WA 1:  No, rat  = final——>C,——>A
    ran                   fan  = initial——>B,——>A
                          bat  = other——>B,——>C,——>A
                                         CA

               WA 2:  No, touch and say ran.
```

Matrix Problem, Part A

```
     an        RR 1:  Good, you have put ran
                      in the cell. Touch and
 r  [ran]             say ran.

               CA:    Good, ran. (——>next problem)
                                        CA
               WA:    No, touch and say ran.
```

Matrix Problems, Part D(30)

RR—Audio-message   CA—Correct Answer   WA—Wrong Answer

If the student makes the correct response (CA), meaning that he touches "ran" with his light pen, he proceeds to Part D where he sees the word written in the cell and receives one additional practice trial. If the student gives a wrong answer, he is branched to a remedial section which will give him practice on initial or final sounds as needed. When a correct response is made, he is returned to Part A. This example shows the possible branching by the computer to give a child extra practice and assistance when he is having difficulty. This is what programmers are referring to when they talk about presenting material on an individual basis and designing a program suited to an individual's aptitudes and abilities. It is rate of progress and amount of practice that is modified.

In the room where the computer-assisted instruction is carried out at Brentwood school, there are sixteen student stations. In the room also are four proctors, three to help children who ask for help, and one to take care of mechanical problems. Unlike the older children in the drill and practice program at Walter Hays, these children at Brentwood figuratively stood in line for proctor help.

In the mathematics tutorial program, Stanford teachers and programmers have the responsibility for the total math program of children. Stanford teachers work in the classroom in mathematics designed to accompany the programmed material. In about twenty-five minutes a day, about one-half is spent in the terminal room and the other half in classroom work. The programmed mathematics is planned at five ability levels:

1. enrich (probably branched out if one mistake made);
2. enrich;
3. ——————→ mainstream;
4. help;
5. help.

Children are branched up or down from the mainstream as their performance is evaluated in terms of right-wrong answers. The branching is usually not recognized by the children. If, for example, a child could not fill in the following numbers in sequence:

10 ___
8 ___
___ 5,

he would be shown a numberline and given problems with it in front of him. Later, he would be branched back to the problems alone.

Patrick Suppes writes, "Immediate correction of a child's errors seems to be an effective teaching device, as does the reinforcement of correct responses. This fact was made apparent in the classroom when the children requested a 'happy face' for each problem they had done correctly"(31). The children had earlier in the reading program been shown a happy face for correct answers or a sad face when the response was wrong. Now they asked for a happy face for each mathematical problem done correctly. To be right is good; to be wrong is sad!

The fixed nature of the programmed curriculum is indicated by comments from a 1967 report:

> By January 1 most children were doing lessons on numeral recognition, counting and N-notation. . . . By the end of March most children had finished the introduction to addition, lessons on sequences, an introduction to the number line, sums through nine, and lessons on open and closed figures, concave and convex figures, and linear measure. . . . Because of severe learning difficulties caused partly by emotional problems and partly by inadequate preparation for first-grade mathematics, a small number of children were given special instruction by the laboratory classroom teacher. These children are now ready to continue with the programmed lessons(32).

The children were readied for the program, not the program adjusted for the children. Is this really providing for individual differences?

Fundamentally, the tutorial programs play a very different and educationally questionable role than the drill and practice program. Conceivably, the drill and practice program could be so germane to the student's classroom concerns that it fit his motivation and needs at a given period of time; that it came when mastery of a skill or basic information would greatly aid him in a larger enterprise important to him. Besides mathematics, this could be true of aspects of spelling and of learning a foreign language. But the tutorial program leads the child all the way, with little opportunity to relate to relevant school or life concerns of the individual. The fact that this is initial instruction in reading is significant. Reading is one means of communication deeply imbedded in the other means—speaking, listening, and writing. To thus isolate and mechanize learning to read strips from it the supporting strength of meaning given when listening, speaking, reading, and writing are related to individual perceptions, images, and concepts in a holistic approach. If the help a computer may be able to give a child in recognizing whole words or in learning phonetic elements is utilized in a manner meaningful to the child, it must be *when* this assists the child in developing a broad stream of reading competencies.

Interestingly, Pauline Sears, a psychologist at Stanford University, is conducting research at Brentwood school with the children working with CAI to discover the effects of CAI on factors other than achievement. Consideration is given to such factors as the sensorimotor skills of the children, the nature of their social interactions, their apparent motivation and absorption in the task, the curiosity and purpose evident in their cognitive behavior. The researchers hope to find out the kind of child who does well in computer-instruction—whether it be the slowest child, the fastest child who races far ahead, the very social child, or some other. This research started with the children in the spring of their kindergarten year and will follow them through the computer-assisted instructional period. Dr. Sears hopes to give followup tests of divergent thinking abilities. After one year of study of the children receiving computer-assisted instruction (CAI), Dr. Sears and her associates did find differences in designated categories of "academic" behavior and "social" behavior. In answer to one of the initially posed research questions, they write:

> Are there changes in children's general classroom behavior over a year which may tentatively be attributed to a partial schedule of computer-assisted instruction? The answer is yes; relative to their non-CAI counterparts, CAI children increased in so called "Academic" behavior and decreased significantly in "Social" types of behavior. Since children receiving normal classroom teacher instruction showed reverse effects, the change does not appear to result only from the effect of six months exposure to first grade, though it must be recognized that the seven classroom teachers (four CAI, three non-CAI) may have exerted influence on this change independent of the computer variables(33).

These researchers suggest that perhaps the non-CAI children developed adaptive patterns of social interaction over the year of group-oriented, teacher-led instruction. By contrast, the CAI children may have been led by the non-social, individualized sessions with the computer to rely less upon the teacher and their peers for reinforcement. They concluded that the provocative results warrant further study.

This and similar research can give us significant data on the performance of children as it is affected by computerized instruction, but it will leave large educational and philosophical problems unanswered. By reinforcing the single-answer approach to education, what happens to the child's total conception of learning? By its very nature, the machine focuses upon the acquisition of correct responses. It disregards the role of questions—the child's own questions—in the learning process. If we wish children to become inquirers and discoverers, other procedures must dominate the educational scene. The machine as used today works against the child's active questioning. Joachim F. Wohlwill makes this quite clear:

> Questions may be a manifestation of the child's active attempts at dealing with the materials and the problems with which he is working, and they may provide him with potentially valuable information. . . . Yet, if there is one thing for which teaching machines as presently designed leave no room, it is the asking of questions on the part of the child. If, to use a favorite analogy of writers on this subject, the teaching machine represents in fact a "private tutor," it is an unbending taskmaster indeed, who can only reply to any question put to it by the child, "I'll ask the questions around here, if you don't mind! On to the next frame!"(34)

Furthermore, immediate feedback may, except in the mastery of skills, be detrimental to depth learning; the arousal of curiosity, imagination, and creativity is of greater significance than satiation in factual information. This is especially true if we want individuals who can go beyond what we know today. Meaningful learning, which allows for depth and reaching forward, stems not from a series of bit learnings struck on by "reinforcements," but rather from a progressive process of cognitive clarification and integration.

The Autotelic Responsive Environment of Omar Khayyam Moore

Most people think of Omar Khayyam Moore's computer-based machine, commonly called "the talking typewriter," as a device to help very young children learn to read or at least to get them ready to learn to read. Dr. Moore thinks of it as a responsive device which placed in a responsive environment will accelerate learning. "The point," he writes, "of using a responsive machine is to change (hopefully to enhance) the emotional or cognitive state of a human being"(35). The machine itself was developed by Moore and Richard Kobler, an engineer from McGraw-Edison Company. The social system conceived as essential to the effective use of the mechanical system is the creation of Dr. Moore who, as a professor of social psychology, uses the theoretical positions and language of social psychology to explain the project.

The autotelic and responsive elements of the environment are part of the social system—"the rules of the game." Activity is to be done for its own sake rather than for obtaining rewards or avoiding punishments; therefore, it is considered autotelic. Moore objects to extrinsic rewards and punishments on the grounds "that they make learning situations unnecessarily complex. In effect, they add relations to be learned"(36). The child has not only the task of mastering a specific learning, but of also figuring out the relation between the reward or punishment and his own efforts.

The responsive environment has been defined as one which satisfies the following conditions:

1. It permits the learner to explore freely.
2. It informs the learner immediately about the consequences of his actions.
3. It is self-pacing—learner determines the rate of events.
4. It permits the learner to make full use of his capacity for discovering relations of various kinds.
5. Its structure is such that the learner is likely to make a series of interconnected discoveries about the physical, cultural or social world(37).

Not all environments are responsive; interactive situations do not fulfill the above conditions. Some freedom of choice must relate to the situation. Children are invited to go to the talking typewriter booth, and they may go or not as they choose; they are left to use the typewriter as they please (at least to begin with); they may leave the booth when they wish. Moore relates these elements of choice to deontic logic—the logic of obligation, permission, and prohibition. He stresses that a situation in which the subjects may refuse to attend, may stay as long as they wish, and leave whenever they wish is very different—deontically different—from a situation in which the subjects are virtually prisoners to the experimental situation.

The curriculum is considered to give equal emphasis to speaking, writing, listening, and reading as coordinate skills, and is described in four phases. Phase I consists of free exploration of the typewriter keyboard. With his finger nails painted with non-toxic water colors in hopes that he will match them to the colors on the keyboard, the child is free to strike keys as he wishes. He can see the letter behind a lucite cover and hear the letter as the machine pronounces it. The machine is set so that no new key can be pressed for about one second so that there is time for the machine to pronounce the letter struck. After a period for exploration and before interest wanes, the child is switched to the next phase. The decision for this is made by the laboratory supervisor. In Phase II, ERE (Edison Responsive Environment) takes the initiative by showing a letter and pronouncing it. At this point, the keyboard is locked so that only that letter can be typed. The child must find the key in a process called search and match. When the child has eliminated all search and can readily match letters, he is considered ready for Phase III or word construction. The machine then confronts the child with several letters at a time—a word. The machine pronounces the word—barn—then the separate letters—b a r n—then the word again. Words are chosen which lead to the reading of a story. In Phase IV, called Reading and Writing, ERE can pronounce a sentence, a paragraph, or a story before or after the child types.

In the fully automated booth, costing around forty thousand dollars, the child is alone and the booth can be monitored from the outside through a one-way window using special controls. Some booths are non-automated; then a booth assistant sits beside the child who has a modified electric typewriter. The booth assistant has a switch to control the typewriter. She is instructed to be as passive as the machine; she can respond as the machine would, but is not to initiate activities. When I visited the Responsive Environment Laboratory in Hamden, Connecticut, I saw only non-automated machines being used although a fully automated machine was available.

At the Responsive Environment Laboratory in Hamden, located in a home owned by the Moores, two groups of children were enrolled. The morning class had thirteen children ranging in age from two to three-and-a-half; eleven 4- and 5-year-olds made up the afternoon class. All of the children could certainly be labeled advantaged. The children were free to stay in the booths up to thirty minutes; the rest of the time was spent in their classroom. By far the largest amount of space, personnel, and, in my estimation, planning was devoted to the booth operation in comparison with the classroom procedures. The classroom was fairly small and not very amply equipped. The only blocks available to these very young children were cheap, lightweight cardboard ones, too slick for effective building. No cubbys or even hooks were available for the heavy winter clothing of the children. When it was time to go home at noon a great heap of clothing was brought into the room. The two-and three-year-olds had to sort through the heap to find their own. Though given some freedom of choice in the booths, I was told the children were made to dress themselves no matter how long it took! The necessary coordination and persistence to cope with heavy winter clothing unassisted are requirements not all two- and three-year-olds have attained.

The morning class had a set routine of outside play or free play indoors followed by snack time, then a quiet time indoors working on number concepts, letters, dice games, etc. When the afternoon group arrived they had their fingernails painted, then a group experience learning Spanish words. They had been studying about China and tasting Chinese food and had pursued a "study" of Africa. Africa was chosen to help a child develop better attitudes toward Negroes. The planning adults expected a "study" of Africa by a four-year-old to change his racial attitudes! This child refused to sit by a Negro child or go with a black booth assistant. The teacher of both groups had formerly taught first grade at Hamden Hall where talking typewriters were first used.

At no place that I visited was I asked more questions about the behavior of children. What about a three-year-old boy who never would allow his head to be bare? He insisted upon wearing a hat or a helmet or a bucket upside down. How about Marion whose grandmother tied her out in the back yard and did not seem to be a very loveable child? The adults at the laboratory seemed hungry for information to help them understand the behavior of children. For among the adults, only the teacher had had any teacher training or any background in child development. The booth assistants were trained merely in that particular procedure.

A good portion of my day was spent in observing booth activities. In the morning group two 3-year-olds wanted to type the names of the other children, for it was getting close to Valentine's Day. The booth assistants showed them, separately, the names in magnetic letters. One girl typed the thirteen names in twelve minutes, while the other worked persistently to complete them in twenty-seven minutes. They were doing very well with search and match stimulated by their own purpose! At least in this instance the booth activity was related to a personal interest of the two girls. One boy whose name began with B typed only B's briefly and left. Another girl typed (matched) and said a number of two-letter words though she reversed some—in (ni). A newcomer of three weeks typed from dictation o, p. q, g and matched from cards u, j. k, b. The youngest child of the group talked about going to a football game with his father. This was taped and he listened to it played back. He typed a few favorite letters before he left. One boy selected the option of not coming to the booth that day.

One child in the afternoon group was enthralled with free exploration of the typewriter with the booth assistant pronouncing the letter—e,e,e,e,; b,b,b,b,b,b,b,; m,m,m,m. But most of the children were working with later phases. One girl was typing words that would get her ready to read a story—play, some, me, thing, jump, train. Her nineteen minutes of typing were interspersed with questions of the booth assistant. "See what I got last night?" (bracelet). "We have only three more." (words). "Why do you have your foot on that black thing?" (the typewriter control). "When I finish can I go downstairs?" (to the classroom). Another girl read a story she had previously dictated and which was written out for her. The story was highly related to the activities of the center:

> She went to school and typed some words.
> She wanted to go downstairs. She was very
> happy, she said. She liked to go to school.
> She typed and was very happy.

The boy considered to be the best reader was reading a book into a tape recorder. He pointed to each word with his finger and read so softly I could not hear much from my vantage point outside the booth.

Though the elements of choice are highlighted in written discussions of the program (and, indeed, they do exist), they do not relate to the vital elements of curriculum content and sequence. The laboratory supervisor or the booth assistants make the vital decisions of moving the child from phase to phase and lead the way by providing sequential stimuli. Most of the process is essentially stimulus-response drill. The autonomy of the child is really minimal—to do or not to do and how long to work at a task. It may even take a personally strong young child to refuse the invitation to go to the booth.

In the children's activities described, there are examples of children speaking, writing (dictating a story), listening, and reading. However, these skills seemed isolated experiences for each child—not related as a "whole" learning experience. Perhaps this is partly due to the age of these children. For three- and four-year-olds, there is frequently not great carry-over from one day's experience to the next.

The conception of learning environments for young children as autotelic and responsive may furnish important guidelines for programs. It may offer valid insights for setting up a total classroom environment. At Hamden it was used only in the operation of booth activities which immersed children into symbolization at a very young age—sometimes even before the age of three. Before they have time for wide exploration and questioning and for building rich and differentiated concepts founded on first-hand experiences, they are placed into an environment which assigns high priority to symbolic elements. A child continuously exposed to letter differentiation in search and match must differentiate between letter forms to master the matching process. In so doing, he is working with segments of a process which can have little meaning for him. He is missing, for example, the meaningful differentiation which can come from play with a good set of blocks with varying size, shape, and weight. In block-building, transferable concepts of differentiated shape can grow with those of size and weight in an initial induction into symbolism which has great meaning for the child. What he builds he understands. This enterprise is replete with functional language, physical and emotional release, creative design, and real autonomy, as well as many other intellectual possibilities. Without doubt, fundamental intellectual growth depends upon the child's repeated interactions with people and things.

Millie Almy relates reading instruction to Piagetian thought in the following manner:

> Many of the implications for beginning reading instruction that emerge from Piaget inspired research have to do with concept formation. To neglect providing many and varied concrete experiences in the period of preoperational thought may later hinder the adequate development of abstract thinking and may possibly interfere with the development of reading comprehension(38).

Can we afford to give priority to a dry husk of symbolism in a program for young children?

Technology in Practice

These uses of technology in the educative process are disappointing in their lack of the extension of the learning environment and in their failure to build relevancy into the learning of young children. Wayne K. Howell, Vice President of the Fund for Media Research in Chicago, Illinois, makes two arresting statements about the use of technology in education(39). First, in discussing a commitment to use media wisely he states, "Important instructional decisions are made at the place of confrontation between teacher and pupil; and, unless the new media and technology can conveniently and comfortably find their place in this confrontation, they will surely not make any constructive difference." In the example of technological instruction just discussed, the machine tended to supplant the teacher rather than being used as an extension of meaningful confrontation. Further, Howell states, "No amount of technology, or specialized media can induce individualized learning unless the student can use the offered information to solve a problem immediately important to him." This element of a personally relevant problem seems essentially lacking in the computerized instruction just described.

The English Infant School

Hearing about curriculum change with a humanistic, personalized emphasis in the Infant Schools in England, I was drawn to explore them personally. So my last trip of the year was to England to visit schools in London and Leicestershire, though these are not the only locations where this change is taking place. The curriculum revolution going on in the primary schools of England cannot be thought of within the theoretical framework which has developed in the United States; other psychological and sociological forces have been at work in England.

In the past, primary education in England has probably been more inflexible than in the United States. For years the insistence that all children take the Eleven-Plus Examination dominated the curriculum and, indeed, children's lives. For at the age of eleven, children were sorted for subsequent educational experiences. Those who were successful on the examination would enter the grammar school with the hope that continuing success could lead them ultimately to a university education. Children who did not succeed on the examination, sometimes estimated at around eighty per cent, could enter secondary modern schools which led either to terminal education at the age of fifteen or to specialized institutions for vocational training. It is obvious that children's concepts of themselves, as well as parental ambitions, were deeply involved. The schools geared all instruction to helping children achieve successfully on the exams. Nowhere was the tyranny of tests more in evidence. Recognizing the emotional traumas caused for children and the adverse educational effects of allowing a test situation to set the goals of education, educators have abolished the Eleven-Plus examination in some geographical areas. Leicestershire led the way in developing a flexible, personalized education which places stress on the meaning of experiences for children. This trend has spread until now, I understand, it includes about 40 per cent of the primary schools in England.

Primary school in England refers to educational units for children from the ages of five to eleven. It has two divisions: the Infant School for children from five to seven years of age and the Junior School for children from eight to eleven. Most of my time was spent in Infant Schools both in Leicestershire and in London, though on two occasions I visited the adjacent Junior School. Infant schools tend to be smaller units than many of our elementary schools, and the headmistress takes on more than the administrative role. She is in direct contact with the children in some teaching capacity. Headmistresses differed in the way in which this was worked out, but it was true in all the schools I visited. In one school, the headmistress took groups for music to free teachers for planning and preparing materials; in another, the headmistress had a room where she worked with reluctant readers, not in drill but in ways to arouse their interest. The headmistress or headmaster in England has great autonomy, not only in his or her own role, but in making decisions about the curriculum of the school. There is an actual freedom for "Heads" and teachers to develop curriculum as it is appropriate for the children in their school. Most repudiate the idea of a prescribed syllabus for all schools.

There are nursery schools, of course, in England; they started there. But financial considerations and the swelling population have limited their expansion. Where they were established as part of an Infant School before World War II, they have continued, but no new ones can now begin at public expense. I did visit two Infant Schools with a nursery school section in economically disadvantaged neighborhoods. Both provided physical care as well as enriched opportunities for play indoors and out, the companionship of other children, and the guidance of trained adults. Some leaders in nursery school education expressed horror at what they had heard about some of the behavioristic projects for very young children in the United States.

A freed English Infant School classroom is a workshop where a wealth of equipment and materials are available for children to use individually for their own purposes. And many are the activities going on simultaneously! On my visits a busy hum of activities pervaded the classrooms, but it was not chaos, for children were moving and talking purposefully and largely independently. In most schools choice and autonomy are so pervasive that a fixed curriculum or a set timetable no longer exists; hence, the term "integrated day". No longer is there a set time for reading, writing, or mathematics. The educational framework and atmosphere bring children naturally to the development of these skills, as they are related to pursuing a larger goal important to the child. Artificial and imposed schedules have been eliminated, thus freeing children to work at an experience for sustained periods of time. In some schools even the morning milk break is unscheduled. Often children in each classroom serve themselves informally without teacher direction as others continue to work. In some schools a central place has been set where children can chat with their friends, frequently from other classrooms, as they drink their daily bottle of milk. At the Water Leys school in South Wigston children come to a central hallway where tables and chairs are set up. Boys and girls take turns serving the milk for a week, two at a time. The servers keep an accurate record of the milk served in number and graph form and record them in The Milk Bar Book. On the day I visited one boy was selling English biscuits to go with the milk and keeping an account of the money he took in.

The integrated day permits a relaxed, purposeful atmosphere in which children can work at their own pace at tasks they have chosen. Time and choice are open to "release and serve children rather than to constrain and prescribe and master"(40). This leads to a great deal of interaction among children who work together in pairs or in small groups. Sub-groups within the class form and re-form as determined by the current ploy. Members cluster around an idea, an activity, or an interest, with opportunity to drift off as other interests demand. Or it may be the teacher who designates a particular small group to work together for a single purpose; perhaps to work on a needed skill in reading or mathematics. Teachers were enthusiastic about the basic flexibility of organization, for they believed it greatly enhanced the learning possibilities for children; it eliminates artificial ceilings for those who learn rapidly; it mitigates the sense of inadequacy children who learn slowly develop in more traditional classrooms. Furthermore, learning is not segmented, but a greater "wholeness" is given to experiences.

Let me describe one Leicestershire classroom. As I walked in I saw three boys with aprons on making chocolate buns. They followed the recipe carefully, mixed the buns, and only contacted the teacher when the pan of buns was ready to be taken to the kitchen to be baked. No one hovered over these children to see that the buns would be a success. The boys moved ahead on their own. Indeed, the teacher reported to me that some days before when other children were cooking they came to her in dismay. After pouring a cake into the baking pan, they licked the mixing bowl and the mixture did not taste good to them. They discovered that they had left out the sugar and the cake was saved.

While the chocolate buns were being mixed, two boys were making a graph of the kinds of vehicles they saw in the parking lot on a recent visit to Bradgate park. Another boy was making a graph of the boys and girls in the class and two adjoining classes. One girl was writing a story to go with a picture she had made about gerbils and using a gerbil book for help with words. A boy was writing a story about birds to go with his own drawing. Four children were making buildings out of cardboard boxes as part of a larger enterprise. At a table of five boys, three were writing in their personal notebooks and two reading together from the Happy Venture Readers. One girl was busily weighing some material on a scale. Some boys and girls were making collages using very shiny paper; a group was building a puppet theater. Other children were out in the corridor painting at easels. Every inch of an Infant School is used to make enriching experiences possible.

The teacher gave advice, listened, for a time devoted her attention deeply to one child writing a story, and moved about as needed. The flexible organization for learning allowed her to be the facilitator of learning and did not require the constant disciplinary measures necessary when groups of children are held to adult-assigned tasks. Indeed, twice in this Leicestershire classroom I saw children settle their own interpersonal difficulties—once over a dispute about who was sitting in a particular chair, again in explaining to me how many gerbils they had had in their class that year. In the latter case, it was misinformation which was cleared up by recourse to the facts which had been written in a book.

This classroom atmosphere naturally draws children into reading and writing. Stories fill their personal notebooks (each child has one from his beginning days in school). Stories relate to school activities, out-of-school experiences, feelings, imaginative adventures. I hardly went into a room where children didn't offer me their written (or for younger children, dictated) stories to read. After their visit to Bradgate Park, a part of Charmwood Forest eight miles from Leicester, one boy wrote:

> On Thursday we went to Bradgate park and Miss Brooks and Miss Holmes and Miss Morton went and there were two buses and we set off at twenty minutes past 9 o'clock. Then we were so excited and we went past the prison and the royal infirmary. I thought the bus was going to brake down but it did not. Thank goodness.

. . . .

> We went up the hill and when the boys got to the top they all shouted Andrews got a girl friend because I was helping Angela to climb the hill. I don't know why they did because its a mans job to help a lady.

Wisely, the teachers put their emphasis upon fluency of expression and the outward flow of ideas rather than upon neatness and absolute grammatical accuracy. Accurate grammar, spelling, and neatness follow as the children's desire and ability to express ideas increases.

Edward Yeomans calls this, education for initiative and responsibility(41). It places great faith upon the autonomous learning of each child—a faith rewarded by the responsible growth evidenced. Most English educators do not want us to think of the integrated day as "a new system" of education, readily transplantable. It is based on a respect for the uniqueness of each child and the commitment to allow for individual differences in all their multifarious human aspects. Thus, it is not expected that one class or one school can pattern itself after another. There are some common strands however: the origin of experiences from the curiosity and concerns of children, the great freedom of choice, the teacher's role as consultant and tutor-guardian, the classroom as a workshop replete with apparatus (the English word for equipment and material). To the unitiated eye Infant classrooms appear to be littered with junk, but these miscellaneous materials serve as stimuli to activities; they aid children to achieve their goals. The key, as in education at all levels, is a teacher who does his best to insure further and wider opportunities—one who can stimulate individual experience and achievement with some degree of individual continuity.

In the many classrooms that I visited the common strands were in evidence, though the actual experiences differed greatly. My observations took me from the dock areas in London to a suburban school in Leicestershire. I shall never forget the Susan Lawrence Infant School on the east side of London where the classrooms were good illustrations of the integrated day. In one classroom particularly, the children were eager to explain their activities for me in broad Cockney! Since it was only my second day in England I had great difficulty attuning myself to their speech, but they were exceedingly patient and we did communicate. They spontaneously repeated a dramatization about astronauts with the elaborate props they had constructed, all for my particular benefit. They explained their rock collections, their graphs, their pictures. They read their stories and showed me notebooks with their sums. One boy was completely absorbed in syphoning water and paid no attention to anything else until he had it working as he wished. Then he came to get me to give me an explanation. The images of these self-directed children remain with me vividly. Of the teacher, significantly enough, I have only a vague recollection—a teacher fostering initiative and responsibility, in fact.

At the Susan Lawrence Infant School, the feeling of freedom with a minimum of physical restrictions permeated the activities. Discipline was there without anarchy; it resulted from a clear sense of purpose on the part of teachers and children. One classroom in the school seemed somewhat hectic as I entered. I would have liked to sit in a corner and analyze the factors bringing about greater volatility on the part of the children. But the teachers expected me and the Headmistress wanted me to visit all the classrooms. This one situation was the exception; in others, children worked industriously and creatively without having prescribed tasks.

What might be considered ideal conditions do not prevail. Every class had forty children for one teacher. Except for one school, built especially for this kind of education, the buildings were old. Some of the best examples of a flexible, integrated day were to be found in a school a hundred years old. Here, at Canonbury Primary School in London, in conjunction with the Infant School, the Junior School operated in the same manner. I was impressed with the achievements of the older children, particularly their depth of study in history, science, and the children's creative expressions. I asked the interesting and vital Headmistress of this Junior school if some children came from the Infant unit without much ability to read. She answered, "Oh, yes, but they have so many other attributes. They like school. They feel all right about themselves and have gained a number of other skills." She tries to arrange to put the children with a teacher particularly able to help in reading skills —not to drill them, but to make reading vital to other enterprises.

In both the Infant and Junior schools the materials and equipment are not designed for mass-produced curricula; they are materials which readily involve individuals or small groups. Many of them are designed by teachers. Vast use is made of unstructured—even waste—materials. Each infant classroom has a Wendy House (a child-sized playhouse), easels, a sand table, a workbench. Water, clay, pets, practical math materials, science stuff, private dictionaries, magnets, scales, mirrors—all are readily available. These plus more precise learning materials are found in the junior school. One classroom, for example, may have Dienes multi-base materials, Nuffield math materials, the Stern blocks and books, and the Madison Project cards for growth in mathematical concepts.

Most of the rooms I visited were vertically grouped—the English term for multi-age groupings. For the Infant School, this meant five-, six- and seven-year-olds together. I saw many instances of older children helping younger children. It was not at all uncommon for an older child to show me what a younger one had done and comment on his good achievement. Peer support, reflecting a largeness of spirit, was part of the learning atmosphere. Admission procedures help to promote this supportive relationship. Children are admitted three times a year, near their fifth birthday. In every class there are "veterans" who can help the newcomers adjust to the requirements of this informal group living.

Of course, performance on a test is not adequate evidence of the effectiveness of this kind of education. However the abilities to gather information, to ask questions, to communicate, or to make suitable choices, for example, are pertinent and open, at least, to subjective evaluation. Barbara Mogford writes that evaluation in Infant and Junior Schools must ultimately depend on the notion of integrity:

> It is commonplace for lip-service to be paid to the notion of all-around development yet in practice this often means sufficient, if biased emphasis on intellectual and physical development, a nodding acquaintance with social aspects of growth, and a glance at, even a shudder at, the thought of emotional development. Integrity of purpose would imply an appreciation by all concerned that schools carry a responsibility for the complete all-round development of the young people in their care. . . . No educational activity is of any worth without a high degree of personal integrity. This demands of those engaged in it whole-hearted and humble respect for persons, an ability to watch progress without making judgments, and an over-riding ability to generate and receive affection(42).

No one in England claimed to me to have a brand new approach to education. Rather, there seems to be a pragmatic but intensely responsible search for meaningful education for young children. In discussing primary education the behaviorists are largely ignored as presenting models too simplistic to be useful in children's learning. The Plowden report contains numerous statements which, in effect, repudiate behaviorism(43). Learning is not laid out for children in minute steps and controlled in each detail. No faith is placed in what Alfred North Whitehead has called "inert ideas" and defines as "ideas that are merely received into the mind without being utilized, or tested, or thrown into fresh combinations"(44). He argues against ideas which at the time they are presented have no bearing upon the child's meaningful activities and do nothing to illuminate and guide his experience. Rather, there is faith that as a child embarks upon an interest in science, singing, or bridge building, he will be introduced to a relevant body of accumulated knowledge and skill which he will share with others who have engaged in the same enterprise.

My visit to England was one of the most fruitful of my entire year. It confirmed the possibility of an education that can help children to be more deeply themselves as well as to learn and to love to learn; hopefully, this will help them to go beyond themselves to deeper levels of identification and broader values. By allowing for the indwelling self to overflow and the outside to be explored from within, competency grows to deal with life as it comes.

Notes

[1]Lucia Johnson, "Inner and Outer-City Pupils Cross Bus Paths in Rochester," *The Christian Science Monitor*, July 3, 1968, p. 3.

[2]Marie M. Hughes, *Early Childhood Research at the University of Arizona Research and Development Center.* Speech presented at a conference sponsored by the Association for Supervision and Curriculum Development on early childhood education. Washington, D.C., November, 1967.

[3]Marie M. Hughes and Jewell C. Taylor, Co-directors, *Why The Project*, Tucson, Arizona: Early Childhood Education Laboratory, University of Arizona, May 10, 1968, Mimeo, pp. 5-6.

[4]Marie M. Hughes, *The Tucson Early Education Model*, Tucson Arizona: Early Childhood Education Laboratory, University of Arizona, January, 1969, Mimeo, p. 6.

[5]*Ibid.*, 2-3.

[6]The program has been extended up to fourth grade and down to kindergarten.

[7]Hughes, *The Tucson . . . Model*, p. 8.

[8]Herbert Sprigle, *A Fresh Approach to Early Childhood Education and A Study of Its Effectiveness*. Jacksonville, Florida: A report submitted to the Carnegie Corporation of New York, n.d., p. 7.

[9]*Ibid.*, p. 30.

[10]*Ibid.*, p. 20.

[11]Madeline Hunter during orientation session before visiting classrooms, September, 1967.

[12]Madeline Hunter, *Nongrading at the University Elementary School at U.C.L.A.* (Los Angeles, California: University Elementary School, University of California at Los Angeles, n.d.), p. 2.

[13]Madeline Hunter during orientation session before visiting classrooms, September, 1967.

[14]Madeline Hunter, "When the Teacher Diagnoses Learning," *Educational Leadership*, 23 (April, 1966), pp. 545-549.

[15]Bernice J. Wolfson, "Pupil and Teacher Roles in Individualized Instruction," *The Elementary School Journal*, 68 (April, 1968), p. 359.

[16]John U. Michaelis, "Social Studies," *New Curriculum Developments* (Washington, D.C.: Association for Supervision and Curriculum Development, 1965), p. 68.

[17]Robert Karplus and Herbert D. Thier, *A New Look at Elementary School Science* (Chicago: Rand McNally, 1967), p. 10.

[18]*Ibid.*, p. 11.

[19]*Ibid.*, p. 21.

[20]*Ibid.*, pp. 20-21.

[21]Science Curriculum Improvement Study, *Material Objects* (Boston: D. C. Heath, 1966). Preliminary Edition.

[22]The first six units were available from D. C. Heath and Company of Boston. In the summer of 1969, it was announced that Rand McNally & Company of Chicago would serve as publisher and distributor of all SCIS units in Final Edition.

[23]Paul McKee, Joseph E. Brzeinski, and M. Lucille Harrison, *The Effectiveness of Teaching Reading in the Kindergarten*, Report of Cooperative Research Project No. 5-0371 (Denver, Colorado: Board of Education, Denver Public Schools, 1966), p. iii.

[24]*Ibid.*, pp. 4-7.

[25]Prepared in the Department of General Curriculum Services, William Spears, Director, *McKee-Harrison Reading Program, Kindergarten—Grade One—Grade Two*. Denver, Colorado: Denver Public Schools, 1964, pp. 3-43.

[26]*Ibid.*, p. 3.

[27]Millie Almy, "Young Children's Thinking and the Teaching of Read-

ing," in *Teaching Young Children to Read*, ed. Warren G. Cutts (Washington, D.C.: Office of Education, U.S. Department of Health, Education and Welfare, 1964), pp. 101-102.

[28]Lloid B. Jones, Report to Board of Education, Denver Public Schools, January 19, 1967, Mimeo, p. 2

[29]E. Paul Torrance, "Factors Affecting Creative Thinking in Children," *Merrill-Palmer Quarterly*, VII (July, 1961), pp. 171-180.

[30]H. A. Wilson and R. C. Atkinson, *Computer-Based Instruction in Initial Reading: A Progress Report on the Stanford Project*. Stanford, California: Institute for Mathematical Studies in the Social Sciences, Stanford University, August 25, 1967, p. 28.

[31]Patrick Suppes, *Stanford Program in Computer-Assisted Instruction*, Progress Report 6 for the period January 1, 1967 to March 31, 1967. Institute for Mathematical Studies for the Social Sciences, Stanford University, Mimeo, p. 5.

[32]*Ibid*., pp. 4-5.

[33]Pauline S. Sears and David H. Feldman, *Changes in Young Children's Classroom Behavior After a Year of Computer-Assisted Instruction: An Exploratory Study*. Stanford, California: School of Education, Stanford University, May 1968, Mimeo, p. 11.

[34]Joachim F. Wohlwill, "The Teaching Machine: Psychology's New Hobbyhorse," *Teachers College Record*, 64 (November, 1962), p. 144.

[35]Omar Khayyam Moore and Alan Ross Anderson, "The Responsive Environments Project," in *Early Education*, eds. Robert D. Hess and Roberta M. Bear (Chicago: Aldine Publishing Co., 1968), p. 176.

[36]Omar Khayyam Moore, "Autotelic Responsive Environments and Exceptional Children," in *Experience, Structure and Adaptability*, ed. D. J. Harvey (New York: Springer Publishing Co., 1966), p. 171.

[37]*Ibid*., p. 170.

[38]Millie C. Almy, "Young Children's Thinking and the Teaching of Reading," in *Teaching Young Children to Read*, ed. Warren G. Cutts, U.S. Office of Education Bulletin, No. 19 (Washington, D.C.: U.S. Department of Health, Education, and Welfare, 1964), p. 101.

[39]Wayne K. Howell, "Technology and the Human Need," *Theory Into Practice*, VII (October, 1968), p. 155.

[40]Roland Barth and Charles Rathbone, "The Open School: A Way of Thinking about Children, Learning, Knowledge," *The Center Forum*, 5 (July, 1969), p. 1. Published by the Center for Urban Education, New York City.

[41]Edward Yeomans, *Education for Initiative and Responsibility* (Boston: National Association of Independent Schools, 1967).

[42]Barbara Mogford, "Ideas on Primary Education," *Ideas* (London: Curriculum Laboratory, Goldsmith College, University of London, March, 1968), p. 5.

[43]Report of the Central Advisory Council for Education (England), Lady Plowden, J.P. (Chairman), *Children and Their Primary Schools*, I (London: Her Majesty's Stationery Office, 1967), p. 192, p. 198, p. 199.

[44]Alfred North Whitehead, *The Aims of Education and Other Essays* (New York: Macmillan, 1959), pp. 1-2.

Directions for Change

Rampant innovations demand constant evaluation using a measuring rod of long-range individual and societal goals. Only as psychological and sociological theory contribute to these goals are they useful to educators.

The Search for a Science of Education

Since the turn of the century some American educators and psychologists have been engaged in a search for educational models or strategies which insure specific learnings by a whole group and permit the precise measurement of outcomes. Economy of time, scientific movement, testing, stimulus-response, aims and objectives —these are labels indicating efforts to bring precision into education. Many are built on the concept of man as passive and amenable to prescribed molding, and on the belief that applicable, general prescriptions (or aims or objectives) can be defined. Scientific research in psychology and education holds immense respect in our country. It is spurred by the demands by foundations or by Congress for measureable proof of progress. For example, proof of increased skill in reading may be requested of a compensatory program when gains may have been more related to increased concentration or improved self-image—the more elusive areas of child growth. But these more elusive gains *are* the first order of business for the educationally deprived child. The complexity of human growth is such that linear progression may be ultimately ineffective. To place young children in situations where the rapid acquisition of reading skills is demanded before these skills have any relevancy may be the poorest way of helping a child become a life-long reader or learner.

Some research patterns applied to young children have been put into a behavioristic, even operant-conditioning, mold, with effectiveness evaluated by reference to a specific performance criterion—usually a gain in I.Q. This is true even though faith in available tests to measure intelligence has waned. Frequently, in visiting projects, it was easier to ascertain the research framework, research techniques, and testing devices used than to learn about the experiences provided for the children. The question of who designed the curriculum was often a revealing one.

Since most of the projects for young children were dealing with the economically deprived, this rather simplistic research pattern was applied to them. Researchers were trying to determine "the match"—the kind of program which would enable disadvantaged children to perform more adequately in school. It was a group search, looking for one program applicable to all children, rather than for "a match" interpreted in individual terms.

Currently, cognitive growth is on the high end of the educational pendulum swing; it is frequently the focus which rides roughshod over other concerns. Cognition tends to be divorced from the totality of human growth in a spurious, injurious manner. By looking at the child only as a knower and failing to utilize what we have learned about him as a reactor and a purposer, many of the newcomers to the field of early childhood education are working ahistorically.

Lack of perspective leads to myopic views. For example, the impact of experiences upon the child's self-image can no longer be ignored. This is a label of consuming interest. However, in project after project I visited, a positive self-image was equated with success in academic areas. Success is important, but a positive self-image is the result of a multitude of factors: physical skills, perceived personal attractiveness, acceptance or rejection by others, tensions, parental relations, cultural expectations. As McCandless defines it, ". . . the self-concept is the apex—the culmination—of all the social and personal experiences the child has had"(1). Preschool education devoted to the nurturing of the individual is only possible as it is built around the nucleus of the self. For the subjective life of the naturally egocentric young child takes pre-eminence.

Efforts at precision and the setting up of direct cause-effect research relationships, as well as lack of perspective and failure to consider long-range human goals, can unwittingly lead to a dehumanized experience for children. Irresponsible research in childhood education disregards accountability for long-term effects. Only by sticking with what is started and facing the outcomes with parents and with the whole community can positive results be expected.

The Value of Theory to Education

The close affiliation between early childhood education and theory in supporting disciplines has both helped and hindered curriculum development. Theories of growth and learning, sincere evidences of man's quest into the unknown, have been essential in giving direction to evolving practice. They have been instrumental in revealing formerly unrecognized realities. But limitations have resulted from accepting theories as scientific facts and from their rigid application to education.

Theories, as found in the behavioral sciences, are just ways of viewing man and the processes of learning. As such, they are but useful metaphors—descriptive in nature. But educators have used them for the prescription of classroom practice. Of the distance between theory and practice Henry Clay Lindgren writes; ". . . the researcher and the teacher have different motives and different interests and live in somewhat different worlds. . . . Because of this gap between the two specialities, it is hardly surprising that research-oriented learning theory has so little to say to the teacher"(2). In summarizing the contributions of learning theory to education, Winfred Hill states, ". . . knowledge of learning theory and related laboratory data provides a worthwhile but also an extremely incomplete background for dealing with the problems of teaching"(3). Many of the truths of psychological theory are but part truths writes Joseph L. Schwab, and "from part truths dependable practical inferences cannot be drawn"(4). He recommends caution in the use of new theory for "about things as complex as the human person and human society, short and simple generalizations must be either empty, false or incomplete"(5).

James Macdonald suggests that we have tried to apply knowledge about human development too directly to curriculum problems. Surely, the use of Gesell's ages and stages led to an erroneous view of groups of children of a specific age level as having homogeneous characteristics. Macdonald considers developental metaphors interesting and reasonably valid within the context of the research done. "When these metaphors," he writes, "are extrapolated and projected into instructional settings they lose a considerable portion of their validity and become much less probable as valid bases for prescribing instructional practices"(6). These educators argue not against the use of knowledge from other disciplines, but for a more cautious application of such knowledge to educational problems. Their plea is for the use of new information within its original validity, and for not extrapolating it for precise educational prescription. Dwayne Huebner refers to new paradigms as "disclosure models," opening up "a world previously unanticipated" and containing "new exploratory possibilities"(7).

In this light, Piaget's theory needs to be viewed. It is descriptive in nature; it does open up new conceptions of intellectual growth and new exploratory possibilities. A teacher knowledgeable in this theory may become much less likely to request a child to perform a mental operation for which he has not developed the necessary prerequisite behaviors. She should, in other words, be able to foster learning experiences which provide a better "match" for each individual child. Used in this manner, the theory may point to greater depth in the curriculum for the young child. But the direct use of this descriptive theory for the prescription of classroom practice may lead to unrealistic closure rather than "disclosure." In the process of translating it to prescription, the application to daily teaching activities, there is the great possibility that some of its validity will be lost. Surely, it should never be used to delineate for the teacher what a four-year-old has to master to become a "normal" seven-year-old. The theory could help to free teachers and children from stereotyped and superficial intellectual teaching in the preschool. It could also become a new cult which is normative and restrictive.

Ira Gordon is quick to acknowledge his transactional model man as metaphoric(8). It is one example of a conceptual realignment growing from newly conceived ways of viewing man and learning. It is of great help in understanding the crumbling concept of fixed intelligence, in discerning the untapped potential of man, and in recognizing man's ever-increasing individuality. It brings us to a realization of the importance of organism-environment encounters in early learning. It enables us to see the young child as active and competence-oriented.

Gordon's model also aids in the assessment of innovations in early childhood education. Most developers of programs designed to help break the deprivation cycle are accepting the notion that development is modifiable and giving credence to the inference that the experiences provided for children in the early, formative years exert a large role in determining intellectual development. Instead of accepting the corollary concept of a child as an active information processor, they hold to a "building-block" view of learning which maintains the concept of the learner as a passive, acceptant organism. Unless programs discard this latter concept, they tend to build toward conformity of behavior and to put limits upon man's self-actualization.

To Gordon's behavioral science model, as helpful as it is, must be added all of man's most expansive thinking to aid in the formulation of a curriculum for children. "To shape a curriculum," Dwayne Huebner contends, "all of man's viable disclosure models must be used—his sciences, his philosophies, his humanities and arts, and his theologies—for the student is too precious, indeed too sacred, to be entrusted to the disclosures of the behavioral sciences"(9). We have failed to acknowledge, as Huebner has pointed out elsewhere, the complexity of man's spirit, and clinging to "oversimplified ideologies foster(s) this misconception"(10).

Humanizing Education

In the broader sweep of human events a great humanist movement is increasingly finding its expression everywhere. The struggle is toward the fuller realization of human dignity and integrity. Internationally it has given rise to the have-not countries and the rejection of colonialism, the work of the United Nations, and the various branches of UNESCO. In our own country it has found expression in civil rights, Head Start, and in other anti-poverty programs. With magnificent vision we hold that poverty can be eliminated and mental health can be achieved by all.

Translated to education this means not only that each learner will be viewed as a person with an individual integrity all his own, but that he will be exposed only to those forces which contribute to self-actualization—self-fulfillment in the broadest sense. In the humanistic idea of man as possessing the potential to select and create a destiny for himself, choice, meaning, autonomy, and creative thinking take priority over atomistic conditioning. Meaning is not only identified with usefulness but with the systematic network that interconnects ideas individually and uniquely. The best assurance of use is learning in situations pertinent and meaningful (interconnected) for the learner. The young child must be guided so that his involvement with the world is deep and personal. Choice and autonomy are more than a matter of when to do designated tasks but of what activities to undertake. There are so many ways to rob a learner of autonomy—use of behavioristic learning model, programming, the process of diagnosis and prescription, the setting of normative standards; yes, even the provision for readiness aimed at the ripening function. How hard it is to have faith in the learner's own autonomy to lead to significant education. Yet, how strong is the desire for self-fulfillment at any age. Creative thinking means reaching out beyond what is already known. It requires keeping curiosity and initiative alive. With commanding impertinence we have declared that intelligence can be created! Our education must allow for this to take place in the context of total self-actualization.

John Gardner writes, "Education at its best will develop the individual's inner resources to the point where he can learn (and will *want* to learn) on his own. It will equip him to cope with unforeseen challenges and to survive as a versatile individual in an unpredictable world. Individuals so educated will keep the society itself flexible, adaptive and innovative"(11). Is this pertinent to the education of young children? Eminently so, for beginnings are of great importance. In the nurturing of the individual, first experiences hold great impact. Also, it is much easier to promote new behaviors that it is to stamp out one set and replace them with new ones. We can easily supply the conditions which make of children the passive receivers of knowledge. Drill, heavy emphasis on skill development, and right-wrong orientations readily kill curiosity and creativity. It is much more difficult to build a day-to-day program committed to broad humanistic goals; but such goals must be a part of programs for young children from the very beginning lest curiosity, autonomy, and creativity be squelched at the source. Unless the great humanitarian principles are applied in early childhood education, the chances are greatly increased for promoting school dropouts.

The holistic, long-range view of growth is evident in some greatly promising projects in our country. A humanizing education was in evidence in the Parent Education Project in Gainsville, Florida, at Nurseries in Cross-Cultural Education in San Francisco, at the Bank Street Early Childhood Center in New York City, and at Tuscon, Arizona in the Cooperative Early Childhood Project. These span the ages from infancy to eight or nine. Not only did these projects support the self-actualization of the young child, but also that of the adults that they touched. Teachers and parents were caught up in the warmth and support of a humanistic education which increased their integrity as persons.

Challenges to Early Childhood Education

Educators selecting humanistic goals for implementation on a day-to-day basis confront three monumental problems in early childhood education—monumental because change involves changing attitudes, beliefs, and behavior of people, and also the bureaucratic school system. First, a humanizing education must be instituted or maintained (as the case may be) throughout the early childhood years, while at the same time helping each individual realize his highest potential. Second, continuity of growth and learning, now sadly lacking, should be possible from nursery school to kindergarten through the primary grades. Third, augmented efforts to help parents understand what constitutes good education for their children and to include them are required.

Continuity in Education

The existing lack of continuity in education in the early years became increasingly apparent to me during my visits to various projects. The primary grades as part of elementary education have adhered to a system of values different from the preschool years. Goals have tended to relate to socially demanded skill acquisition. Indeed, the immediate acquisition of reading skills by all six-year-olds, though completely at odds with what we know about individual differences, has become a fetish. With a separate history and differing goals, the nursery school and some kindergartens have stressed social and emotional development, though many of our best nurseries and kindergartens have provided well for intellectual growth. No partial aspects of growth should, of course, constitute a complete program for children. Nor can we afford to allow one segment of a child's education to negate the development of earlier years. All too often what has been gained in nursery school, kindergarten, or Head Start classes in ego development, fluency of language, creative expression, cooperative abilities, or a host of other personal or social growths have been neglected or even reversed in primary grades.

The falsely dominating skill values in many first grades are being pushed down to younger children. The newly recognized intellectual potential of the young child is being misinterpreted as allowing for a new timetable of symbolic language and skill learning.

Instead of creatively searching for fresh stimuli to learning, investigators are succumbing to the temptation to push down reading and writing experiences to younger and younger children, thus extending the belief (really a myth) that to do things earlier is better.

If what Piaget and others have told us is right, this is the wrong direction to take in providing challenging stimuli. His theory discloses that it is through the manipulation of their physical environment and in social encounters that children extend, differentiate, and combine action images and correct intuitive impressions of reality (space, causality, time). As the child assimilates impressions and accommodates to a large variety of first-hand situations, he builds the foundations of logical thought. An expanded variety of encounters is necessary to build a foundation of breadth and depth. This is as true of six- and seven-year-olds as it is of five-year-olds. How then can we continue to allow the sharp dichotomy between the kind of experience a child has in kindergarten and that found in most first grades? Free social interaction, manipulation of materials, and a wide range of first-hand experiences are essentials in all of early childhood education.

The absence of continuity in the education of the young child has troubled early childhood educators for some time. A search for ways of eliminating this discontinuity was evident soon after kindergartens started in the United States. As early as 1887, Kate L. Brown told members of the National Education Association meeting in Chicago, "The kindergarten as a separate, isolated fact, will never be more than a pallid little blossom, that scarce knows whether to live or die"(12). She recommended that the kindergarten and the primary school work in sympathy with each other. Lucy Wheelock believed Froebel's principles of development provided a means of bringing about continuity and stated, "The ideal relation of the kindergarten to the primary school is only possible when the guardian of each looks upon her particular stage of school life as a part of a continuous process, and plans her course from the standpoint of universal principles of development"(13).

Ultimately, three practical means were utilized to unify the work of the kindergarten and first grade: the preparation of teachers knowledgeable about education at both levels, the designing of curricula encompassing both, and the utilization of one school supervisor for kindergarten and first grade(14). A survey of teacher training institutions between 1924 and 1926 revealed eighty per cent preparing teachers for both kindergarten and the primary grades. The survey describes a reorganization within the U.S. Bureau of Education in 1925 to create a section of nursery, kindergarten, and primary education "in keeping with the general movement to unify the work for all ages of young children"(15). The new curriculum books of the 1920's encompassed kindergarten and first grade(16).

As we approach the last decades of the twentieth century, however, we find no greater educational discontinuity than that which still exists in the early childhood years. In all their sincere efforts, early childhood leaders failed to recognize the obstacles a teacher faced, even though she was supplied with training in both educational levels and with curricula which made unification possible. Teachers, singlehandedly, or even with the help of sympathetic supervisors, could not reverse the dichotomous values and traditions which even now create a gulf between the kindergarten and first grade.

Innovations today are more numerous in the preschool than in either public school kindergartens or in the primary grades. Besides reflecting changing theory, this may evidence the greater possibility for change in classrooms outside the bureaucratic structure of American schools. In institutionalizing the values and traditions of the primary school which are decades old, the system holds teachers, children, and their parents in the grip of outmoded beliefs. Public elementary schools have been organized with fixed roles for teachers and administrators to the point of forming a system resistant to change. I am reminded of the statement by J. L. Meriam in 1916 that "there is serious danger that organization works to the advantage of system, but at the sacrifice of the boy and the girl"(17).

School organization does not need to be regimented and inflexible. It can be more simply conceived as a group of people working together for the education of children. This more simple conception impressed me in the English Infant schools I visited. Schools in general were smaller units with fewer children—though not fewer children per teacher. Headmasters and headmistresses had intimate knowledge of what went on in the school and of individual children. The "Heads," as they call themselves, worked directly with children at times in a teaching-learning relationship and worked closely with teachers in discussing curriculum and preparing new materials. Such an atmosphere of searching together for the good of children opens the way for change.

One further aspect of the organization of many English Infant schools eliminates discontinuity in the education of five- and six-year-olds (though it may produce discontinuity later on). Non-graded classrooms of five- to seven-year-olds allow for the continuous growth of each child over this span of years. Any emphasis on sequence, inherent in subjects or skills, is replaced by continuity of growth which can be thought of only in terms of an individual child. Only then can real continuity of learning develop. Multi-aged classrooms in the United States hold the promise of placing the focus upon the continuous growth of each child as a person.

As early childhood education reaches increasingly downward into infancy and to parents, continuity over all the years of early childhood needs fresh consideration. Not sequences of knowledge, but continous growth and learning for each child deserve fundamental attention. Not the child readied for an inflexible school curriculum, but the school ready to take children and provide "the match" necessary for optimum growth. Some of our new disclosure models should aid us in this task.

A Humanizing Curriculum

With the teacher working day after day with one group of young children rests the exciting challenge of providing an educational setting which will make operational stimulating, sometimes disturbing, new theoretical ideas. In the midst of many sterile kindergartens it takes a creative teacher and supportive administrators to envision and operate a program which will not only develop a fundamental relatedness with and among children, but also feed their intellectual yearnings. Such a program was in operation in the kindergarten at the Nueva Day School in Menlo Park, California where children were learning through all of their senses—touching, smelling, tasting, hearing, seeing—in a classroom where learning is considered an adventure. Two days a week this kindergarten group cooks their own lunch at school and stays through the lunch hour. At the end of each week the children take home a one-page report of their activities of special interest. In the early weeks of the year these contain sketches (no words) which help them recall and relate their experiences to others. These pages could only be "read" by the children involved. By November of 1967 one week's page had the words *Humperdinck*, *Moussorgsky*, *Plymouth*, *'tween decks*, and *hold* along with the sketches for recall. During my visit I observed a busy clean-up time in which children took the responsibility for putting all things in their accustomed places and sweeping the floor, a lively discussion about Pilgrims, and a time for creative rhythmic expression. The teacher reported that earlier in the year these children from upper socio-economic levels were very self-conscious and unfree in their bodily movements. By November they readily participated in dramatic expression, giving evidence to the priority accorded this in the curriculum. Not only was curiosity and creativity kept alive in this kindergarten, but new dimensions were fostered.

Considering the pressures for rapid skill acquisition and the inflexible hold of age-grade standards, it takes vision, cooperation, and diligence to devise a more humanistic program for children in the primary grades. The early childhood program at Tucson is an illustration of such vision. As a cooperative endeavor between the University of Arizona Early Childhood Education Laboratory and the public schools of Tucson District No. l, it appears to be breaking old normative molds and conceptualizing growth in a broader perspective. The program for children is not subordinate to tradition, but freer to relate to more meaningful learnings and successful achievement, thus eliminiting the established patterns of early school dropouts.

The complexity of making operational on a day-to-day basis the best we know for children is recognized by those designing new programs. Young children have to have a balance between vigorous motor activities and quieter moments. They require individual and small-group situations. They depend upon significant adults working together—parents, teachers, aides, pediatricians. They need an expanse of space indoors and outdoors with adequate equipment and materials to challenge them and keep curiosity alive. They must have spontaneous and planned experiences which utilize their deep motivation to understand their world. They require a program that fosters intellectual growth.

The need for integrating intellectual and affective growth is readily apparent. Programs exist which provide emotional support but blandly fail to challenge children intellectually. The many instances I observed of the child's emotional well being sacrificed for intellectual gains reveal the opposite problem. A reconciliation of knowledge of development in all realms is requisite.

At the very heart of curriculum planning stands the problem designated by Hunt as "the problem of the match." This is a restatement in the field of cognition of a dilemma long recognized by educators. How can the expanding inner reality of the young child relate to the outer realities of life around him? In his writings, Froebel frequently referred to the child's making "the inner outer and the outer inner"(18). He regarded development as proceeding from the connectedness between the child's inner strivings and an absorption—a taking in through the senses. In the same vein, William Rhodes writes about psychosocial learning that the school needs to serve a more "effective mediator role between the internal dynamics of the individual and the external dynamics of the society"(19). For education, an act of human influence, to bring the individual to the outer world of public truth with full respect for the private reality of inner experience is an awesome task.

A recognition of the pre-eminence of the subjective, egocentric life of the young child leads us to attend much more to the inner dynamics as a basis for learning experiences. A taking in of outer reality comes only as the young child perceives its relatedness to him. It comes essentially through sensory-perceptual-motor channels. Only as these experiences form a rich background for understanding the outer world is the child freed from dependence on first-hand experience so that symbolic representations become an added means of learning. In Piagetian terms the child's thought gradually becomes decentered from perception and action. It is only when thought is decentered at about the age of eleven or twelve that truly abstract thinking is possible; that logical deductions and generalizations can be made without reference to empirical evidence. In the early years, before this is attained, the varieties of materials needed for breadth of experience should be conceived only in the broadest of practical limits. Activities which involve the child in perceiving and conceptualizing are most essential.

The child's use of symbolism expands gradually over a long period of time. It begins with symbolic play in which the child projects his "interiorized images" of people, situations, and objects. Play enables him to test, clarify, and reconstruct his inner schemata in the light of additional perceptions. Painting, block building, and construction of objects at a workbench are all initial forays into symbolization and are steps toward more abstract symbols. Some children readily make the transition to the use of words and letters; for others, this transition is more difficult. A depth to the child's growth in cognition may be added as he gains skill in categorizing, seriating, projecting, recalling, or generalizing. A teacher's knowledge of Piaget's work can be an invaluable aid in this direction. The work with "kits" of related objects in the Tucson Cooperative Project is promising in its contributions to more abstract thinking.

Can we select experiences for young children better than they can for themselves? I saw no evidence of this being true. Too often I saw the attempts to channel the learning of young children result only in limiting learning possibilities. Attempts to offer growth-inducing experiences became pressures which tried to insure a specific learning for all children. There is perhaps a fine line between offering a gentle challenge and overwhelming children into compliance. Equilibration, the process Piaget considers pedagogically fundamental, is relevant here. A transitional mechanism, continuously operating between the growing child and his environment, reconciling assimilation and accommodation, it depends upon self-regulation and self-correction. Consider Piaget's forceful statement:

> In the realm of education, this equilibration through self-regulation means that school children should be allowed a *maximum* of activity on their own, directed by means of materials which permit their activities to be cognitively useful. In the area of logico-mathematical structures, children have real understanding only of that which they invent themselves. Thus, there is no good reason to try to accelerate this development too much; the time which seems to be wasted in personal investigation is really gained in the construction of methods(20).

So few investigators have grasped the educational implication of Piaget's insistence upon the active role of the learner. Few also have captured the tremendous significance of Ira Gordon's conception of the transactional model man as an open-energy, self-organizing system developing a uniqueness continuously evolving from organism-environmental transaction. When the active role of the learner is grasped in all its implications, it will be recognized that more is involved than physical freedom in the classroom or than the pacing of experiences to individual rates of growth. Since no two learners of a given age or grade are at a single developmental level, the variety of choices requisite extend to choices among stimuli or encounters and problems to be solved. The learner helps select the problems to be solved, setting up goals and evaluating their attainment. This is learning how to learn. In the best English Infant classrooms I visited, choice and involvement goes this far.

If we put together this knowledge about how children grow and learn with the long-range goals of optimum, satisfying, personal growth and a continuous, humanizing education, what does this demand of education for young children? First it requires enriching environments from infancy. We must move from a false, compensatory concept to a mandatory downward extension of education, though not necessarily institutionalized. The compensatory model defines deficiencies and plans direct means of eradicating these in a linear fashion. The rapid growth of compensatory programs threatens to arrest early childhood education at the stage of the compensatory models. Rather, from the beginning stages of growth, an environment is needed which takes care of children, keeps them alive, and makes them grow. It should include continuous interaction between persons, materials, ideas, performances, and objects—not divorced from life, not removed to verbalizations—but related to the life of the child. The barriers between institutionalized learning and life outside must be broken down. The young child must experience life directly until symbolism becomes relevant to life for him. This is true not only of the preschool but of the primary years. The best guarantee for this type of humanizing education is individualization, even personalization, of the curriculum where the child can initiate tasks and become personally involved and self-directed.

Some few new projects are leading the way, and new materials and equipment are being created which support individual manipulation and involvement. Nurseries in Cross-Cultural Education show how the technology of our day—typewriters, cash registers—can provide materials for manipulation. The Tucson Project uses the community of the child as an area of exploration and the expansion of concepts. These are the directions with promise for rich conceptual growth, meaning, and relevancy. The classroom environment of the young child, a man-made environment as all classrooms are, must offer a wealth of wide-ranging experiences in school and in the community in which he can manipulate, create, investigate, and reproduce in dramatic play and in the creative arts. Alexander Frazier explains the varieties of support from adults necessary to maximize learning from the exploration of resources: ". . . respect for and use of the exploratory impulse found in physical activity in general and play in particular; provision of many opportunities for manipulation of and experimentation with the items and events of the immediate environment; regularization of the processes of becoming progressively more accurate in identifying these items and events by name, setting up categories in terms of their attributes, and classifying new items and events as encountered; and a continuous concern for the role of socialization and interaction in the whole range of learnings"(21).

A relatively stable, non-graded group of peers is a necessary part of the young child's educational setting. Language is sharpened for better communication. The joys of literature and art may be enhanced in a group matrix. In the interactive context of the group, self-concept grows. The non-graded aspect of the group will expand the kinds of relationships possible in the group. In classrooms in the English Infant school, I found seven-year-olds supporting the endeavors of five-year-olds and five-year-olds respecting the accomplishments of older children. In other classrooms, I found children working together in small mixed groups unaware of age stratifications.

Does this kind of environment contribute to "the match"? Does it mediate between the private reality of inner experiences and the outer world? It holds much greater possibility for doing so than the life in classrooms where teacher direction and right-wrong orientations predominate. This man-made curriculum environment, so appropriate to the young child's nature, allows for his selection among stimuli. Yet, it provides for eliciting, shaping, and relating possibilities. These mediating possibilities are designed by James Macdonald as he explains, "The eliciting of behavior must go far beyond the narrow social and intellectual responses encouraged in most young children's programs. It must extend to areas of sensitivity, aesthetic response, mental potential, and human activities which provide for wholeness"(22). The shaping of behavior, under these conditions, comes in full recognition of the crucial role of learner control of stimuli. Freedom, choice, and responsibility within ethical relationships will build toward those modes of behavior recognized as essential today—authenticity, autonomy, and commitment. Hopefully, these will grow along with behaviors with content—cooperation, courtesy, orderliness. For fostering persons who live consistently with authenticity and integrity, not persons who profess one set of values and live by another set, these guidelines are essentials in their education from its beginning.

A Community of Supportive Adults

Children need many adult role models in order to develop a balanced conception of adult participation. In the nuclear family of today, divorced as it is from continuous contact with the extended family, children develop close affiliations with only two adults—sometimes only one. The need of the child to have a number of supportive adults who convey to him that they really care about him as a person can, at least, be more generously met at school. This, of course, demands more male figures in the education of the young. Interested laymen, as well as professionals, can contribute to children's well being and future attainments.

Children can only profit when there is a unity of aims between the school and the home. The opposite tends to be true not only in ghetto areas but in affluent suburbs. The goals of the more traditional education with which parents are familiar are at odds with a humanistic, individualized education. New procedures for working together are called for to help parents understand the values of newer educational conceptions. Formalized meetings for "parent education" will never achieve a unity of aims. Lecturing and telling do not develop a working relationship or eliminate basic distrust. To accomplish a unity of aims we must turn to the best we know about group processes and bringing about change. Authenticity, support, and relevancy must characterize relationships with parents as well as children.

Teachers and the Opening Classroom Door. Nursery school teachers have never worked alone; for the safety and health of the very young, more than one adult has been deemed necessary. Depending upon the kind of nursery school facility, teachers have worked cooperatively or as head teacher and assistant. But there has seldom in the past been more than one adult in a kindergarten or primary classroom; a closed-door policy has prevailed. A reversal of this policy can profit the community, parents, children, and the teacher herself.

If a teacher is conceived as a person committed to growth and change in her teaching role, she needs continuous support. In the projects I visited where teachers were supplied with challenging new procedures and materials together with the basic rationale, a vital spirit pervaded the classroom. When changes coincided with the teacher's own humanistic tendencies and at the same time supported her growth, her receptivity to further changes increased. Such was true of many classrooms in the Tucson Cooperative Project where the teachers had developed a faith that they were doing something significant. There was an intangible spirit which gave vitality to the classroom which the teachers were willing to share.

The use of aides is opening the classroom further to more adults and frequently constituting a link with the community. At the Pre-Kindergarten Demonstration Center in Rochester, the director was warm in her praise of the effectiveness of the aides in the program. The aides supplied much information about children. They were a link to the parents most difficult to reach. They also worked in the classroom, not to do just the cleaning up, but to assume expanding roles as members of the teaching team.

Parents as Partners. Parents need to be drawn closely into the educative process for at least two reasons:

1. Education begins in infancy and only as parents and teachers work together can a continuously fruitful education result for each child.

2. Only with the support of parents can the educational values discussed become universal.

The recognition of the importance of education beginning in infancy creates a corollary recognition: the need for a more potent relationship among the significant adults in a child's life. Early education cannot exist in isolation from the total environmental situation—economic, social, and emotional—in which the child interacts on a continuing basis. A more vigorous interaction between adults of the home and adults of the school milieu would set up a mutual influence to bring the two most formative environments of the young child closer together. This means an involvement of parents in the educative process as it is meaningful to them and their children. The Parent Education Program in Gainesville, Florida demonstrates the way in which this can be done with the parents of infants. The Bank Street Early Childhood Program exemplifies a program enhancing parents' effectiveness and involving them in their child's school life.

Parents need to be made partners in demanding and promoting a personal and relevant education for each child. Otherwise, their adherence to the false myths of traditional education erect a formidable barrier to change. Nurseries in Cross-Cultural Education and the Bank Street Early Childhood Center are effectively developing a positive image of what a school is, what teachers can do, and how parents can involve themselves in their children's significant learning. These, and other programs working similarly, are leading the way in building a positive partnership with the economically disadvantaged parents of children enrolled.

Just such a partnership is equally necessary with parents in more affluent areas. This may be even more difficult to achieve because parents of the middle- and upper-class levels are strongly tied to age-grade standards and the early learning of overpublicized symbolic skills. Precise activities for these parents will need to be altered, but many of the characteristics of the programs successful at other social class levels are basic essentials. A growing sense of trust and mutual respect built around the best each adult can give to the child is fundamental. In the New York and San Francisco programs, two procedures prevailed: 1) starting with parents where they were, with the goals and aspirations they had achieved, and 2) an open-door policy which allowed parents to learn about their child's program in school and the reasons for it. This open-door policy did not mean hoards of adults going through classrooms or teachers acceding to all manner of demands from parents. It meant the welcoming of parents to the school setting for more than a few planned meetings. It meant welcoming them as respected members of the enterprise and involving them meaningfully so that they felt good about their child's school. The first time I visited a school in Newton, Massachusetts, a parent spontaneously said to me, "This is the most wonderful school for children and parents. Parents are welcomed to their child's class." The parent had just finished reading a story to four young children. This meaningful involvement in the work of the classroom augmented her positive feelings about the school.

Early childhood is the time to develop this partnership. The focus must be the child, not the parent's or educator's ego-involved goals for the child, but the communication of a deep. honest concern for the child. Teachers can contribute professional skill and knowledge about curriculum. Parents can contribute their information about their child's growth. Both can bring the social realities of life today to bear upon the curriculum.

Notes

[1]Boyd R. McCandless, *Children: Behavior and Development* (New York: Holt, Rinehart and Winston, 1967), 2nd ed. p. 254.

[2]Henry Clay Lindgren, "Theories of Human Learning Revisited," in *Behavioral Science Frontiers in Education,* eds. Eli M. Bower and William G. Hollister (New York: Wiley, 1967), p. 183.

[3]Winfred F. Hill, "Contemporary Developments Within Stimulus-Response Learning Theory," in *Theories of Learning and Instruction*, ed. Ernest Hilgard, Sixty-third Yearbook of the National Society for the Study of Education (Chicago: University of Chicago Press, 1964), p. 53.

[4]Joseph J. Schwab, "On the Corruption of Education by Psychology," *The School Review*, LXVI (Summer, 1958), p. 181.

[5]*Ibid*., p. 184.

[6]James B. Macdonald, "Myths about Instruction," *Educational Leadership*, XXII (May, 1965), p. 574.

[7]Dwayne Huebner, "Implications of Psychological Thought for the Curriculum," in *Influences in Curriculum Change,* eds. Glenys E. Unruh and Robert R. Leeper. (Washington, D.C.: Association for Supervision and Curriculum Development, 1968), p. 31.

[8]Ira Gordon, "New Conceptions of Children's Learning and Development," in *Learning and Mental Health in the School*, eds. Walter B. Waetjen and Robert R. Leeper (Washington, D.C.: Association for Supervision and Curriculum Development, 1966), p. 50.

[9]Huebner, *Influences in Curriculum Change*, p. 32.

[10]Dwayne Huebner, "Curriculum as a Field of Study," in *Precedents and Promise in the Curriculum Field*, ed. Helen F. Robison (New York: Teachers College Press, 1966), p. 98.

[11]John W. Gardner, *Self-Renewal* (New York: Harper and Row, 1965), p. 26.

[12]Kate L. Brown, "Application of Froebel's Principles to the Primary School," *Journal of Proceedings and Addresses of the National Education Association*, 1887, p. 339.

[13]Lucy Wheelock, "Ideal Relation of Kindergarten to Primary School," *Journal of Addresses and Proceedings of the National Education Association*, 1894, p. 702.

[14]Evelyn Weber, *The Kindergarten: Its Encounter with Educational Thought in America* (New York: Teachers College Press, 1969), pp. 114-115.

[15]Mary Dabney Davis, *Nursery-Kindergarten-Primary Education in 1924-26*, Bulletin No. 28 (Washington, D.C.: U.S. Government Printing Office, 1927), p. 2.

[16]See for example, Samuel Chester Parker and Alice Temple, *Unified Kindergarten and First Grade Teaching* (Boston: Ginn, 1925). Agnes Burke, *et al.*, *A Conduct Curriculum for the Kindergarten and First Grade* (New York: Charles Scribner's Sons, 1923).

[17]J. L. Meriam, "Practical Means of Unifying the Work of the Kindergarten and the Primary Grades," *Journal of Addresses and Proceedings of the National Education Association*, 1916, p. 430.

[18]Friedrich Froeble, *Education of Man*, trans. William N. Hailmann (New York: D. Appleton, 1889), pp. 5, 55. *Pedagogics of the Kindergarten*, trans. Josephine Jarvis (New York: D. Appleton, 1895), p. 119.

[19]William C. Rhodes, "Psychosocial Learning," in *Behavioral Science Frontiers in Education*, eds. Eli M. Bower and William G. Hollister (New York: Wiley, 1967), p. 228.

[20]Jean Piaget, "Foreword," in Millie Almy, *et al.*, *Young Children's Thinking* (New York: Teachers College Press, 1966), p. vi.

[21]Alexander Frazier, "Curriculum Making for Children: Elements and Issues," in *A Curriculum for Children*, ed. Alexander Frazier (Washington, D.C.: Association for Supervision and Curriculum Development, 1969), p. 5.

[22]James B. Macdonald, "A Proper Curriculum for Young Children," *Phi Delta Kappan*, L (March, 1968), p. 408.

Index

M. Rakatine